# Pirates

Written By Joanne Mattern
Illustrated By Chris Marrinan

ROURKE PUBLISHING
Vero Beach, Florida 32964

www.rourkepublishing.com

PHOTO CREDITS: © Manley620: © JGroup: Title page; © Lagui: © Manley620: © JGroup: pages 4, 5, 26, 27, 28, 29, 30, 31, 32; © Library of Congress: pages 26, 27, 28

Edited by Katherine M. Thal
Illustrated by Chris Marrinan
Art Direction and Page Layout by Renee Brady

**Library of Congress Cataloging-in-Publication Data**

Mattern, Joanne, 1963-
  Pirates / Joanne Mattern.
     p. cm. -- (Warriors graphic illustrated)
  Includes bibliographical references and index.
  ISBN 978-1-60694-433-2 (alk. paper)
  ISBN 978-1-60694-542-1 (soft cover)
  1. Pirates--Juvenile literature. I. Title.
  G535.M3775 2010
  910.4'5--dc22
                              2009020493


Printed in the USA

CG/CG

www.rourkepublishing.com - rourke@rourkepublishing.com
Post Office Box  643328 Vero Beach, Florida 32964

# Table of Contents

## Freddie

Freddie is a cabin boy on the ship called the *Providence*. He is seeking adventure on the high seas and finds it with *Calico Jack*.

## Peter

Peter is a sailor on the *Providence* who teaches Freddie about life on a ship.

## Mary Read

Mary Read joins *Calico Jack's* ship with a secret. Anne Bonny discovers her secret and becomes her friend.

# Anne Bonny

Anne Bonny is as fierce as any male pirate. She maintains the respect of the other pirates and becomes friends with Mary Read.

# Calico Jack

Calico Jack is the captain of his ship. He treats his crew fairly, but can be vicious when necessary.

Note: The characters and events in this book are based on real pirates and their adventures. However, the story itself is fictitious.

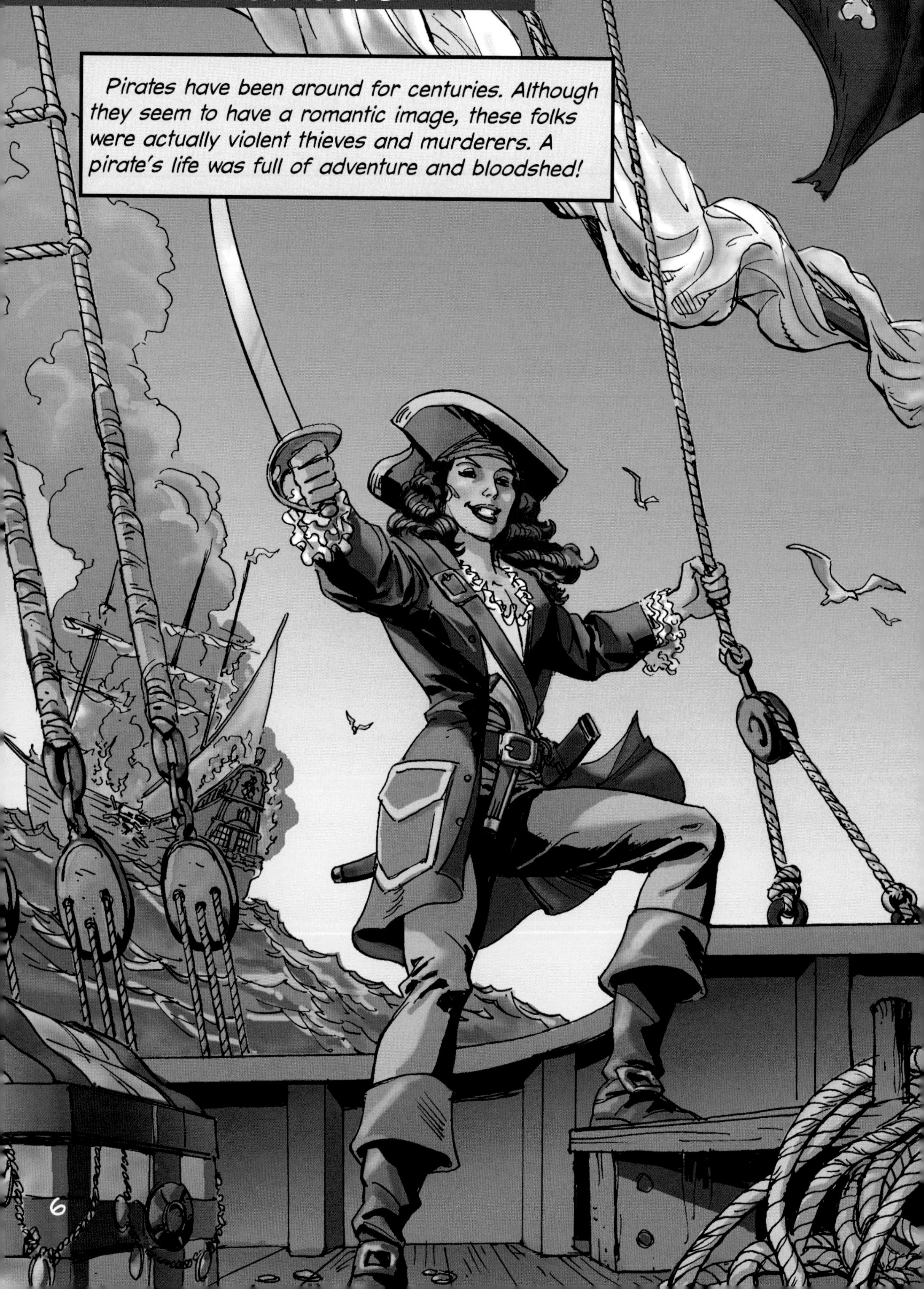
Pirates have been around for centuries. Although they seem to have a romantic image, these folks were actually violent thieves and murderers. A pirate's life was full of adventure and bloodshed!

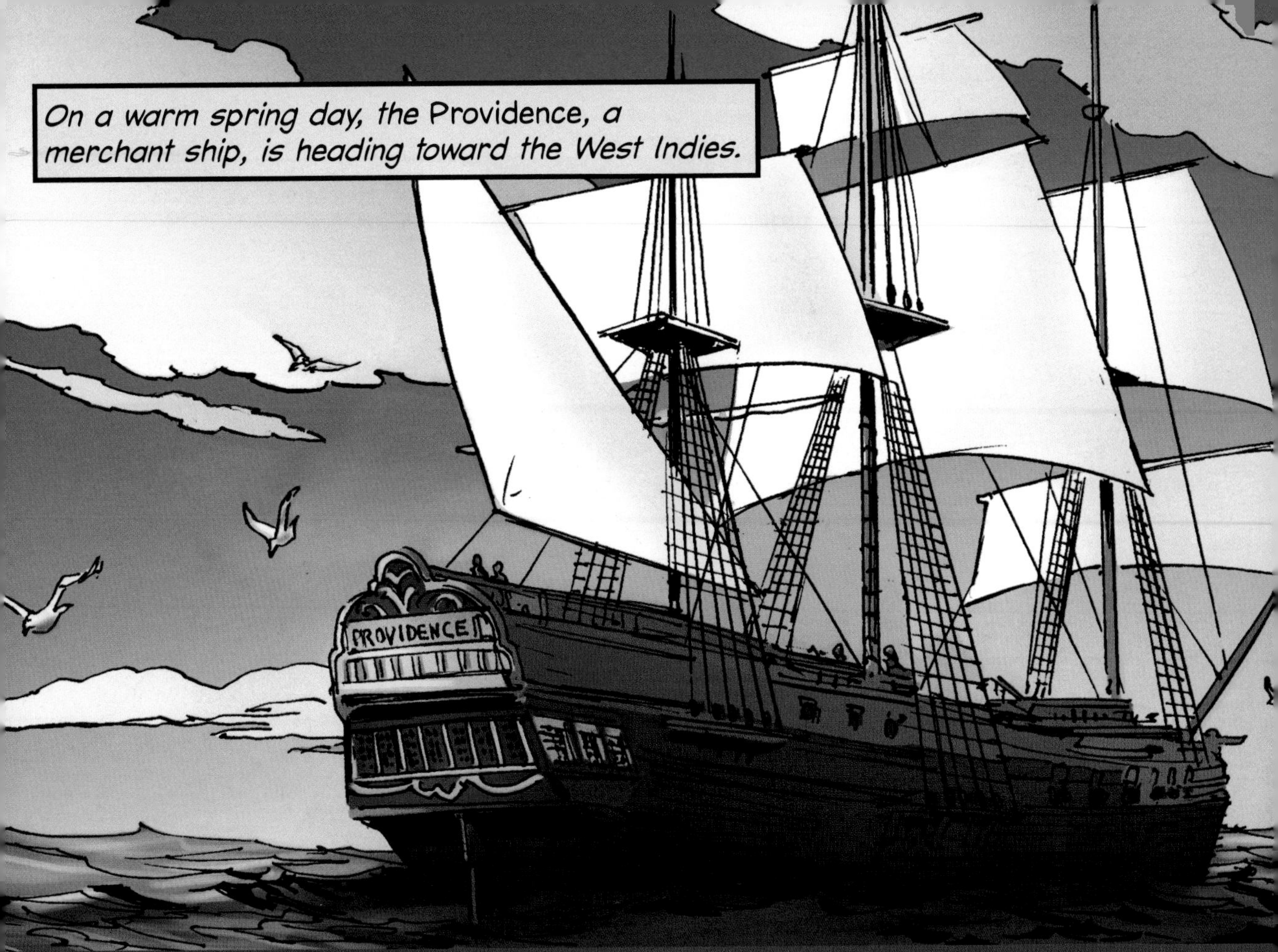
On a warm spring day, the Providence, a merchant ship, is heading toward the West Indies.
PROVIDENCE

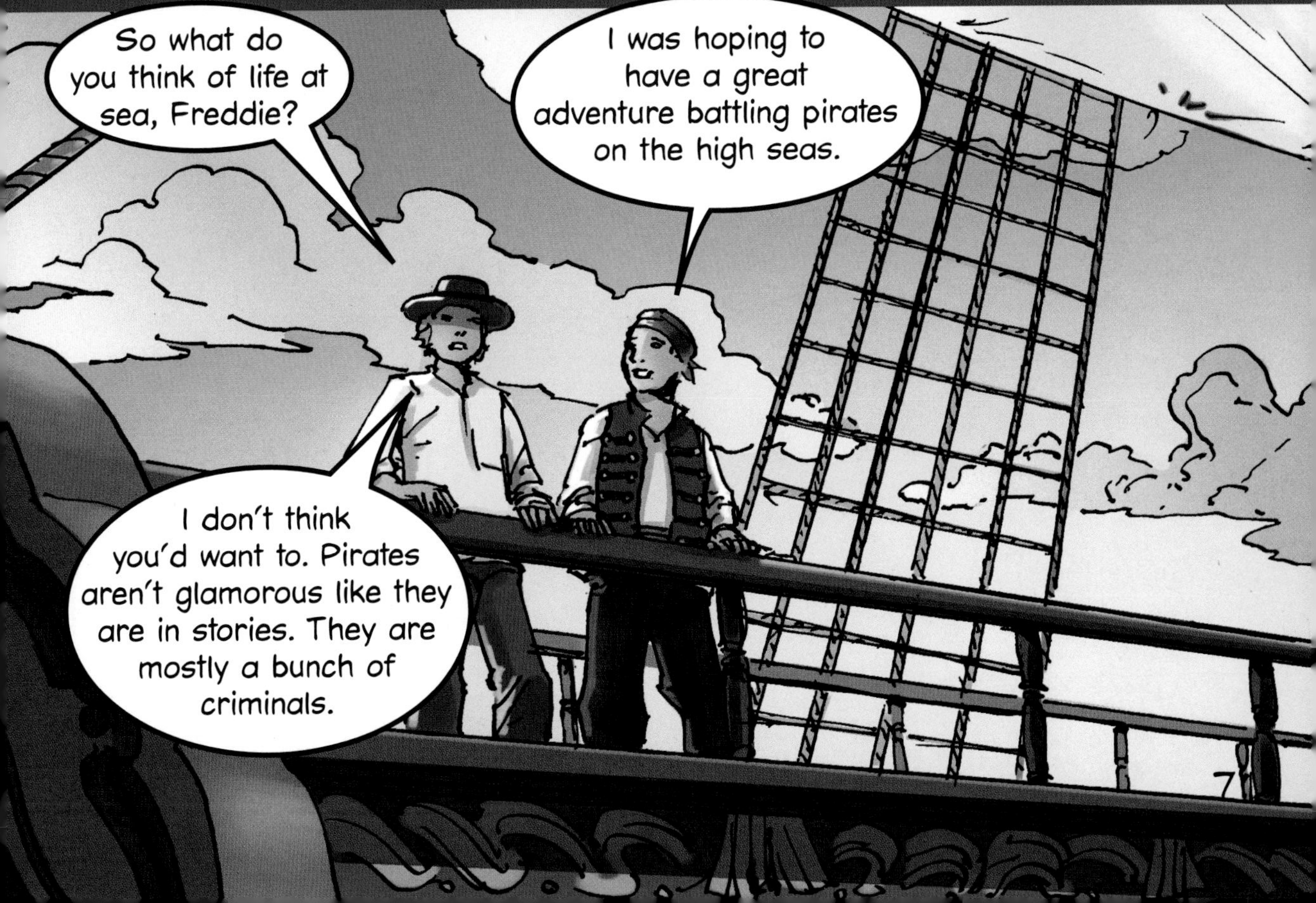
So what do you think of life at sea, Freddie?
I was hoping to have a great adventure battling pirates on the high seas.
I don't think you'd want to. Pirates aren't glamorous like they are in stories. They are mostly a bunch of criminals.

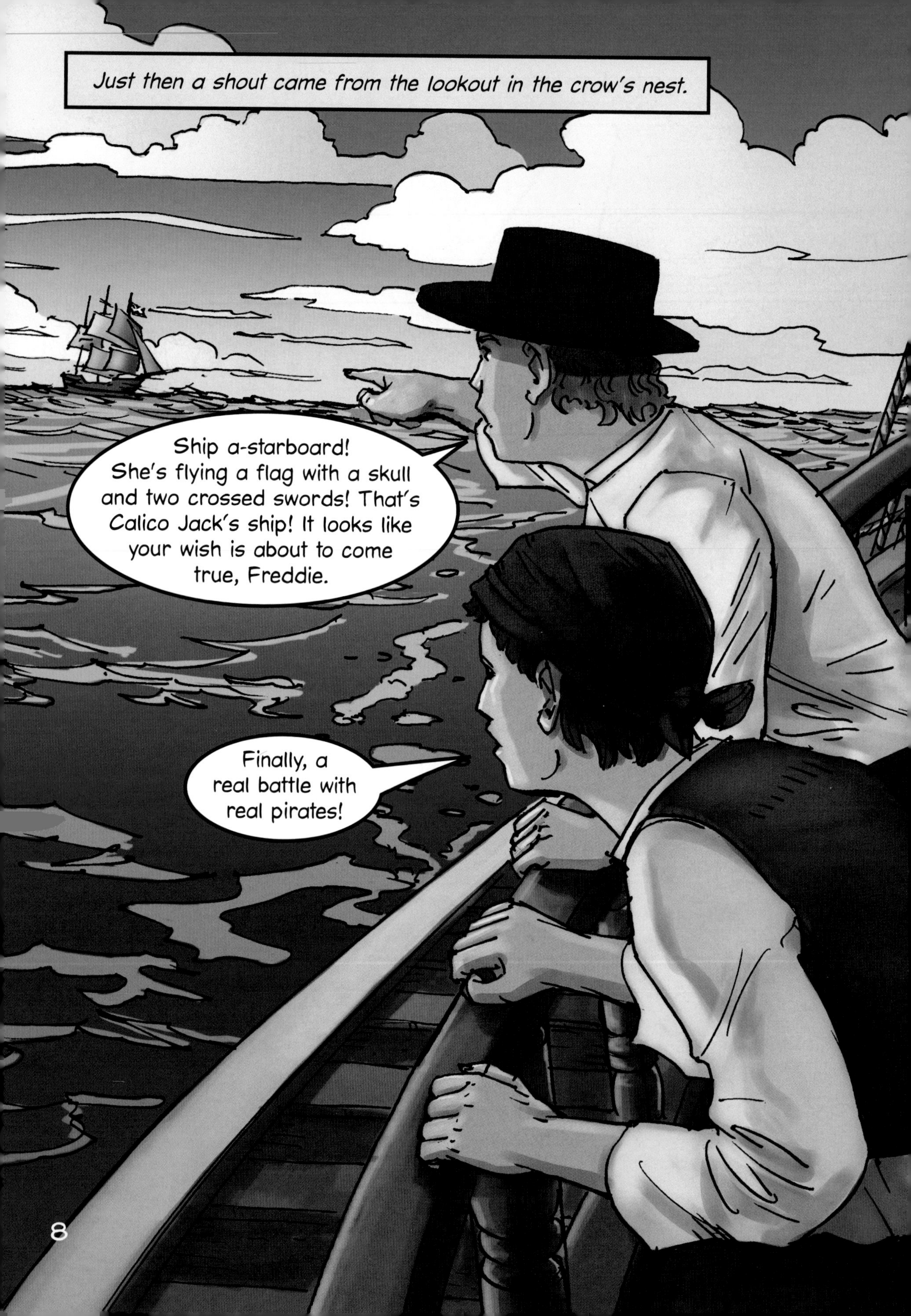
Just then a shout came from the lookout in the crow's nest.
Ship a-starboard! She's flying a flag with a skull and two crossed swords! That's Calico Jack's ship! It looks like your wish is about to come true, Freddie.
Finally, a real battle with real pirates!

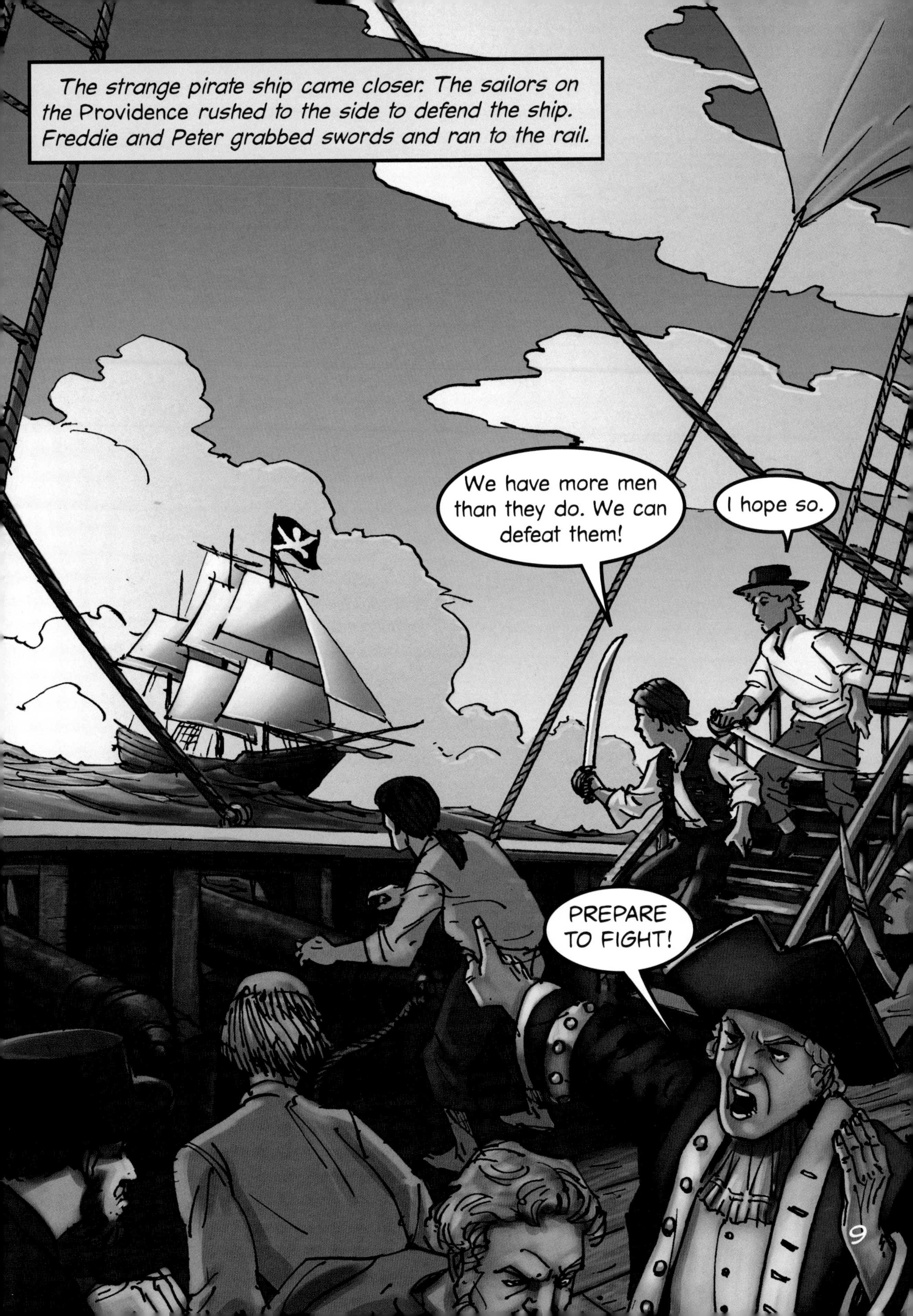
The strange pirate ship came closer. The sailors on the Providence rushed to the side to defend the ship. Freddie and Peter grabbed swords and ran to the rail.
We have more men than they do. We can defeat them!
I hope so.
PREPARE TO FIGHT!

# CAPTURED BY PIRATES

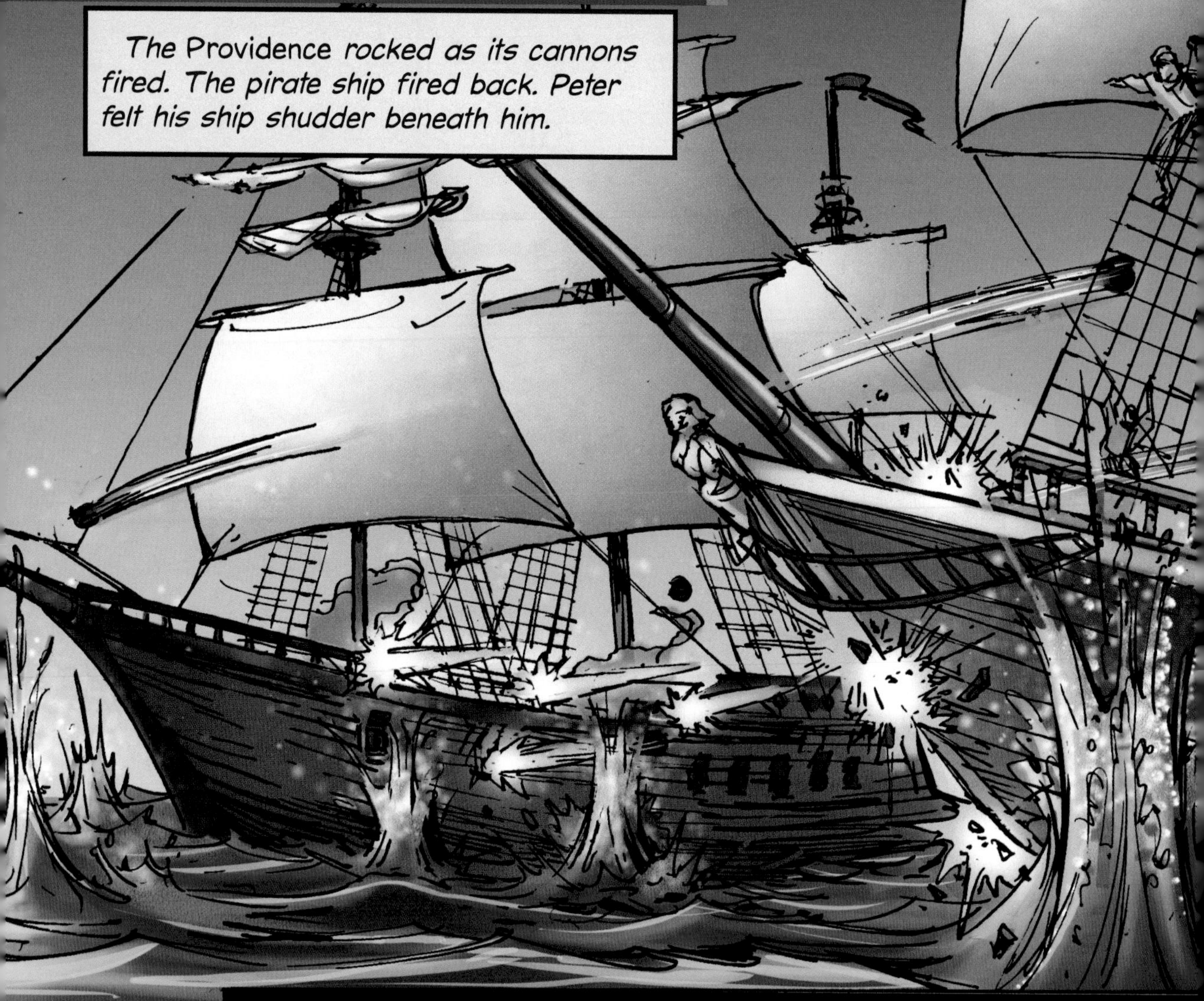
The Providence rocked as its cannons fired. The pirate ship fired back. Peter felt his ship shudder beneath him.

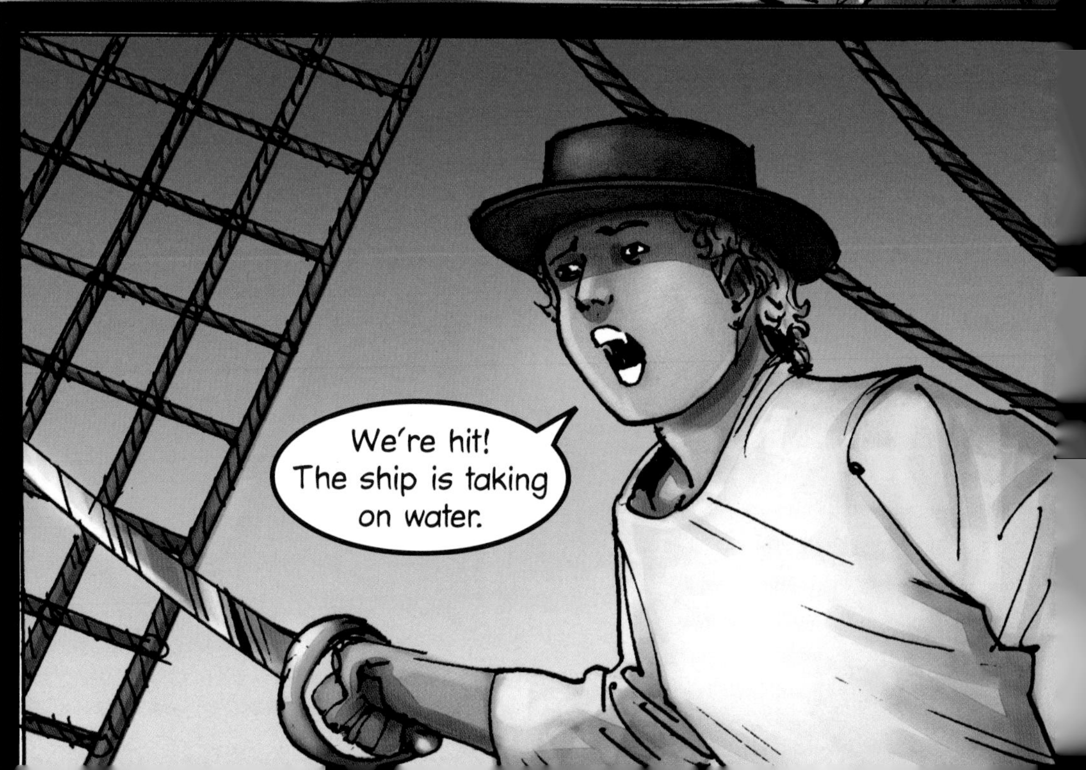
We're hit! The ship is taking on water.

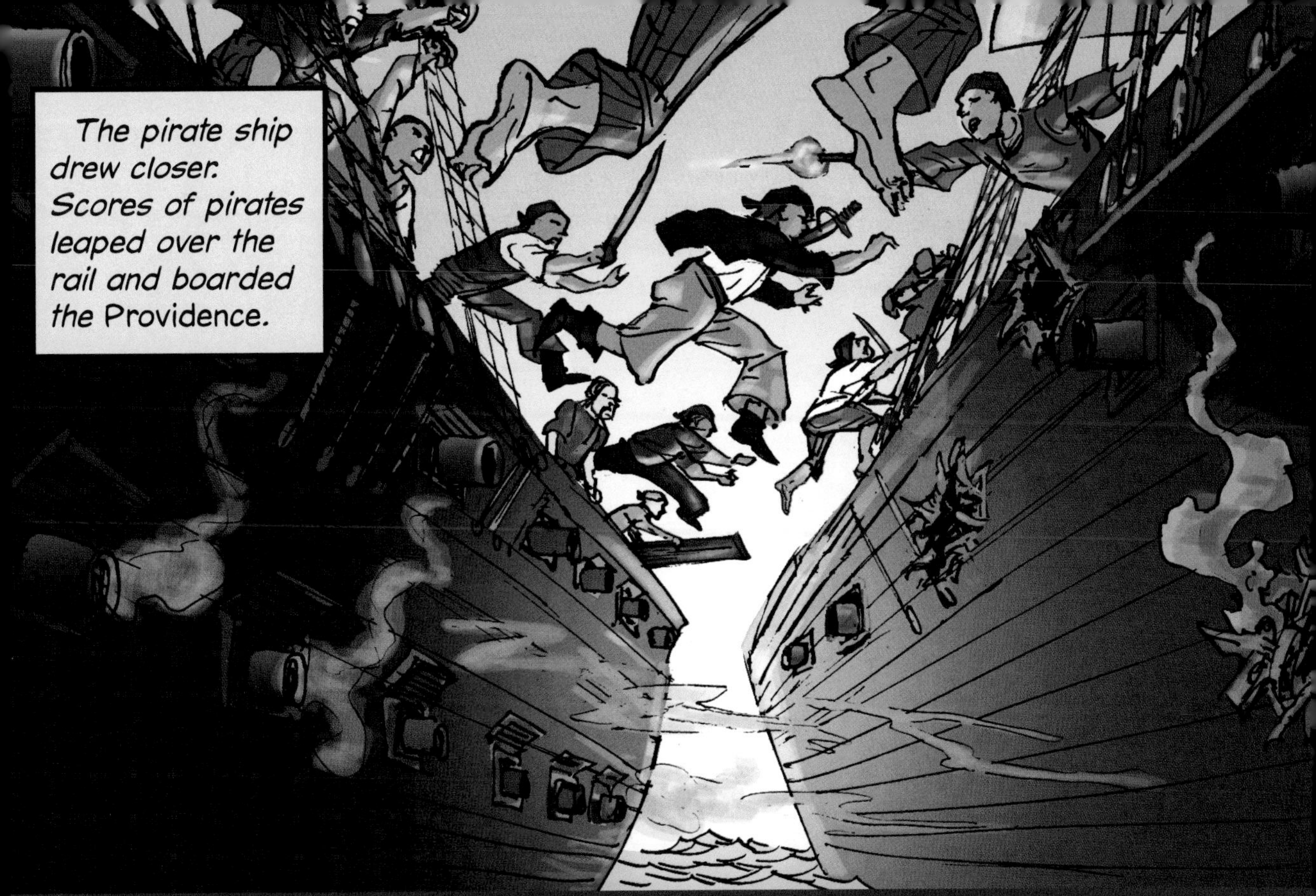
The pirate ship drew closer. Scores of pirates leaped over the rail and boarded the Providence.

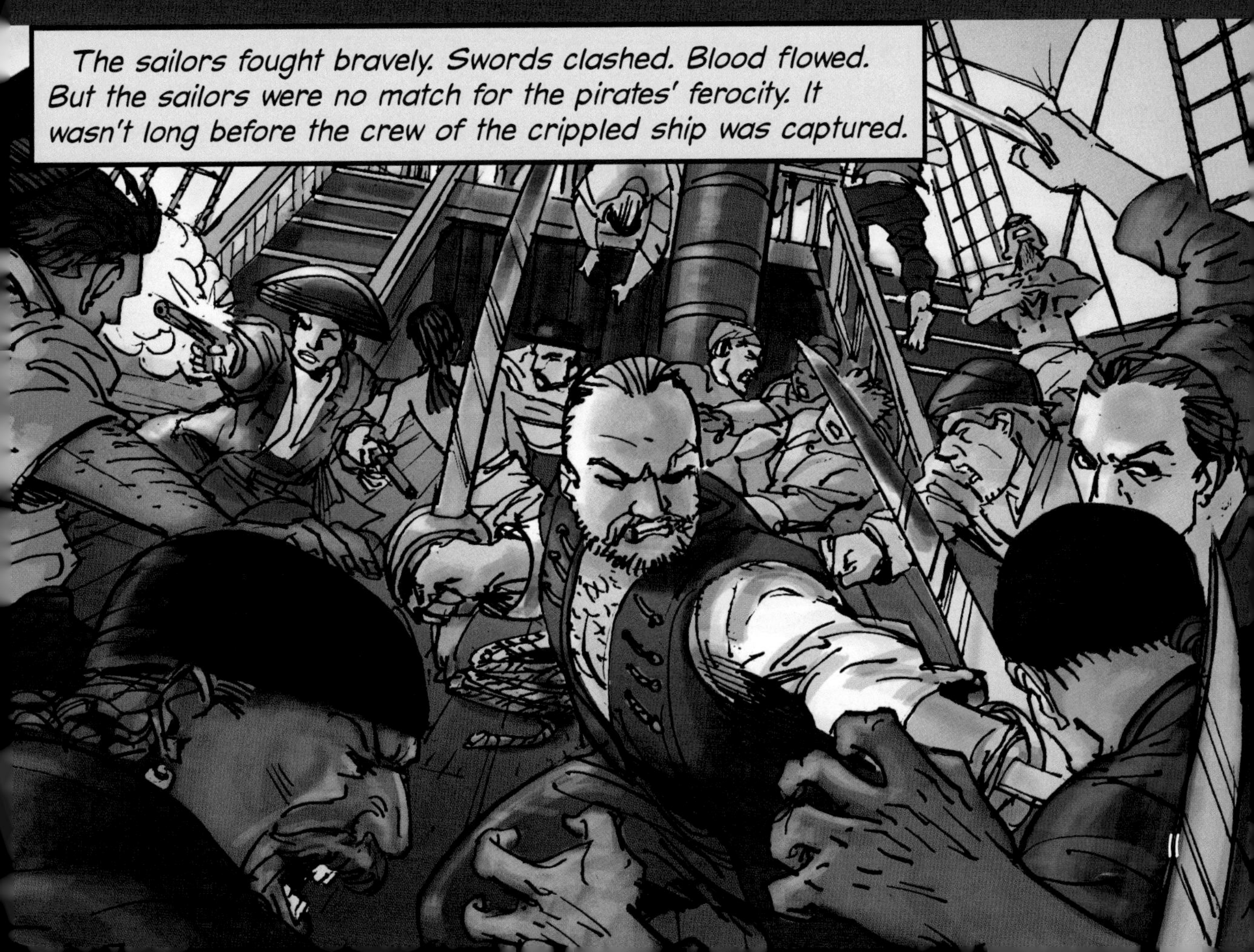
The sailors fought bravely. Swords clashed. Blood flowed. But the sailors were no match for the pirates' ferocity. It wasn't long before the crew of the crippled ship was captured.

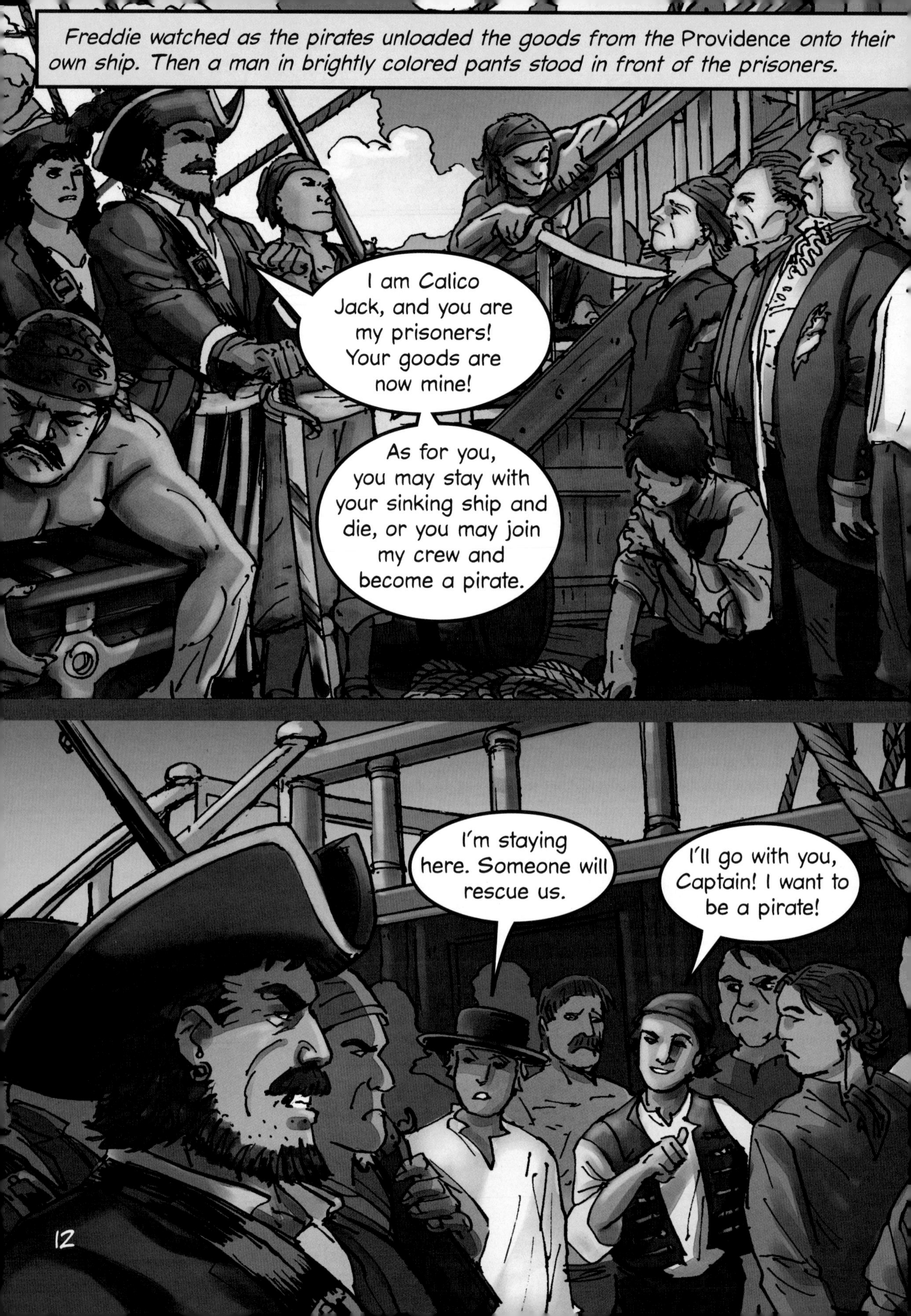

Freddie watched as the pirates unloaded the goods from the Providence onto their own ship. Then a man in brightly colored pants stood in front of the prisoners.
I am Calico Jack, and you are my prisoners! Your goods are now mine!
As for you, you may stay with your sinking ship and die, or you may join my crew and become a pirate.
I'm staying here. Someone will rescue us.
I'll go with you, Captain! I want to be a pirate!

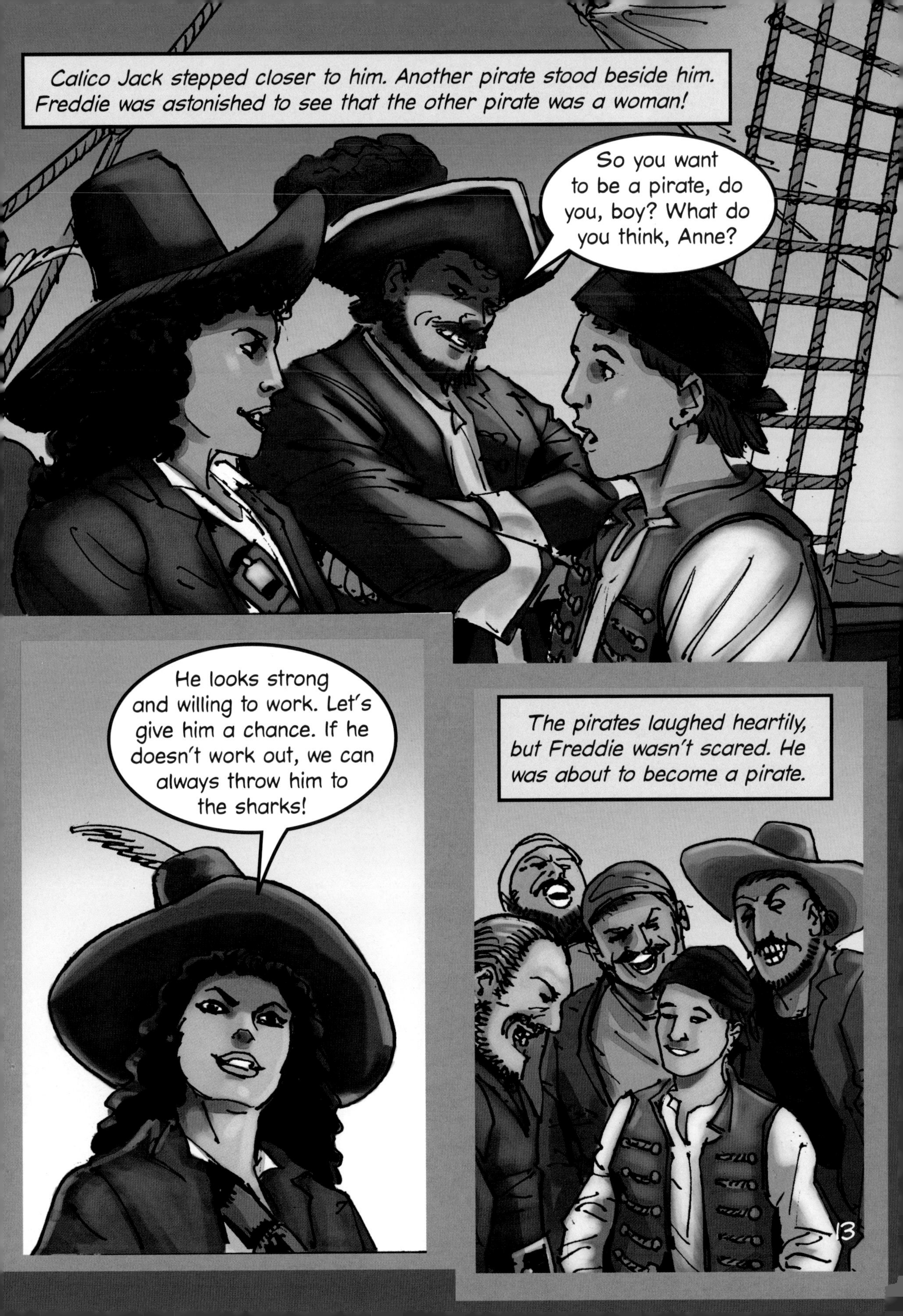

Calico Jack stepped closer to him. Another pirate stood beside him. Freddie was astonished to see that the other pirate was a woman!
So you want to be a pirate, do you, boy? What do you think, Anne?
He looks strong and willing to work. Let's give him a chance. If he doesn't work out, we can always throw him to the sharks!
The pirates laughed heartily, but Freddie wasn't scared. He was about to become a pirate.

# A PIRATE'S LIFE

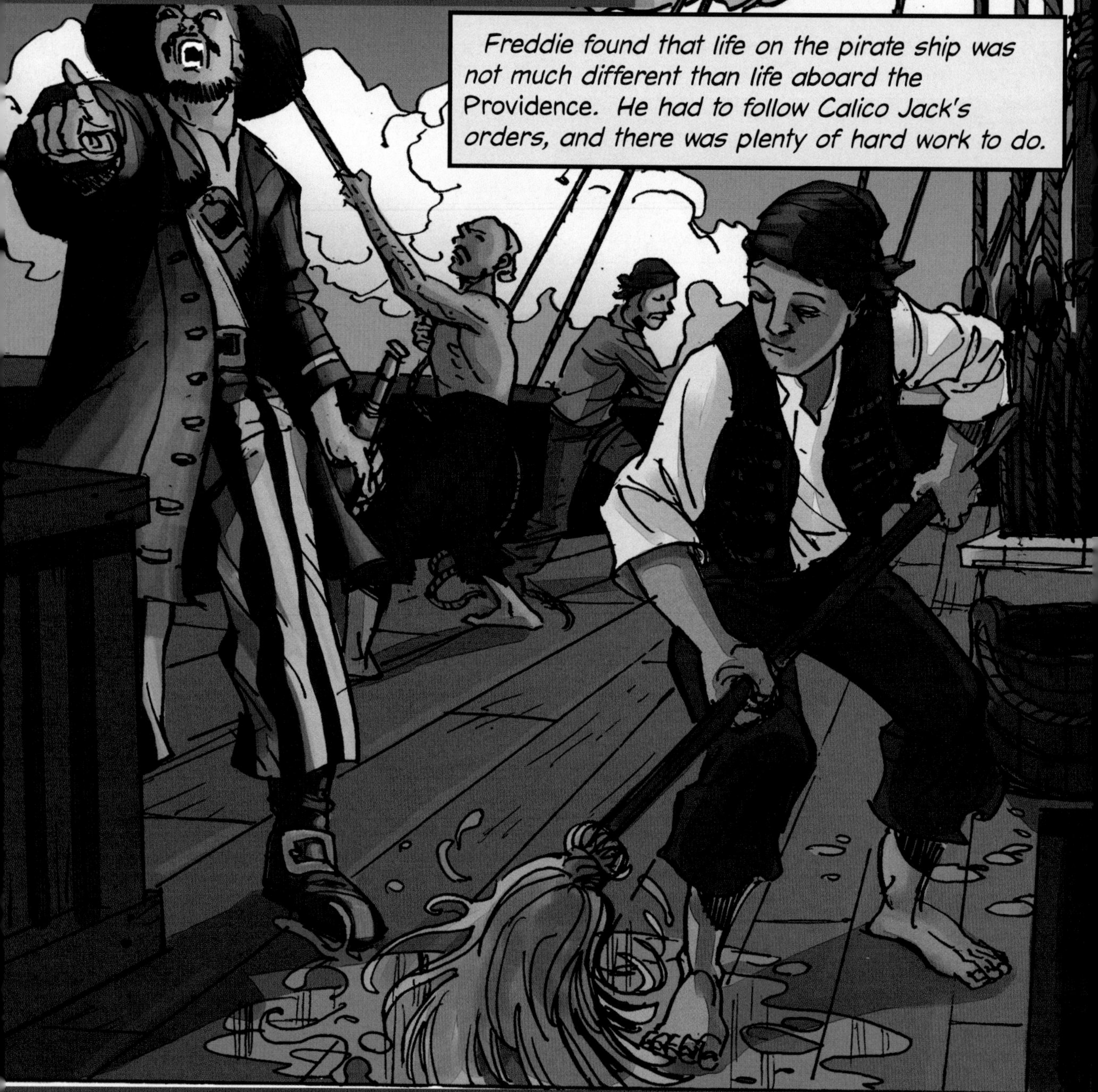
Freddie found that life on the pirate ship was not much different than life aboard the Providence. He had to follow Calico Jack's orders, and there was plenty of hard work to do.

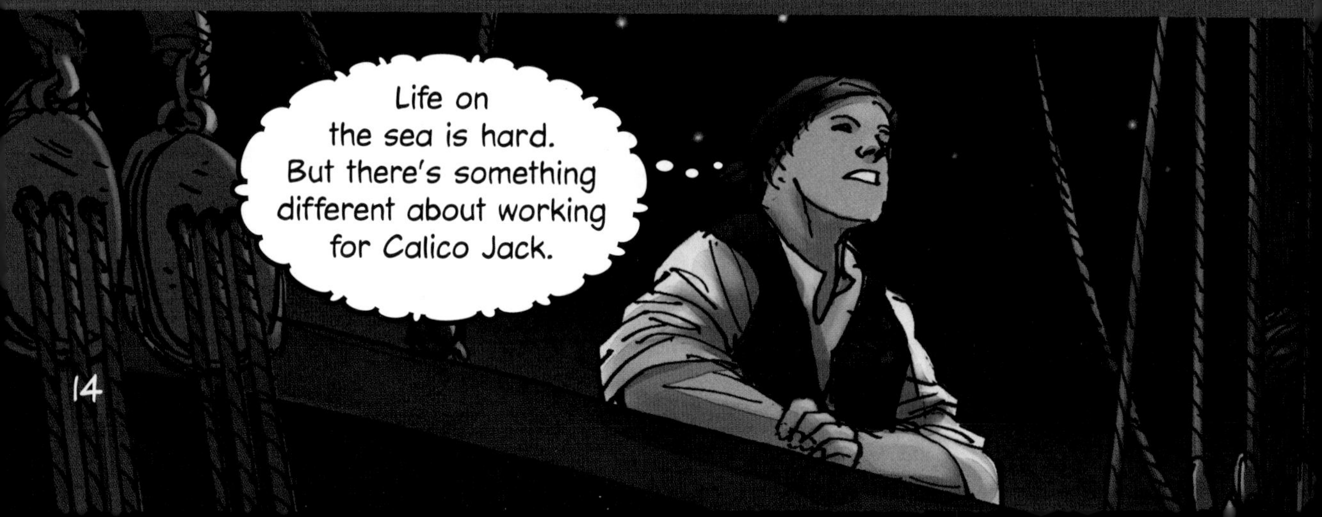
Life on the sea is hard. But there's something different about working for Calico Jack.

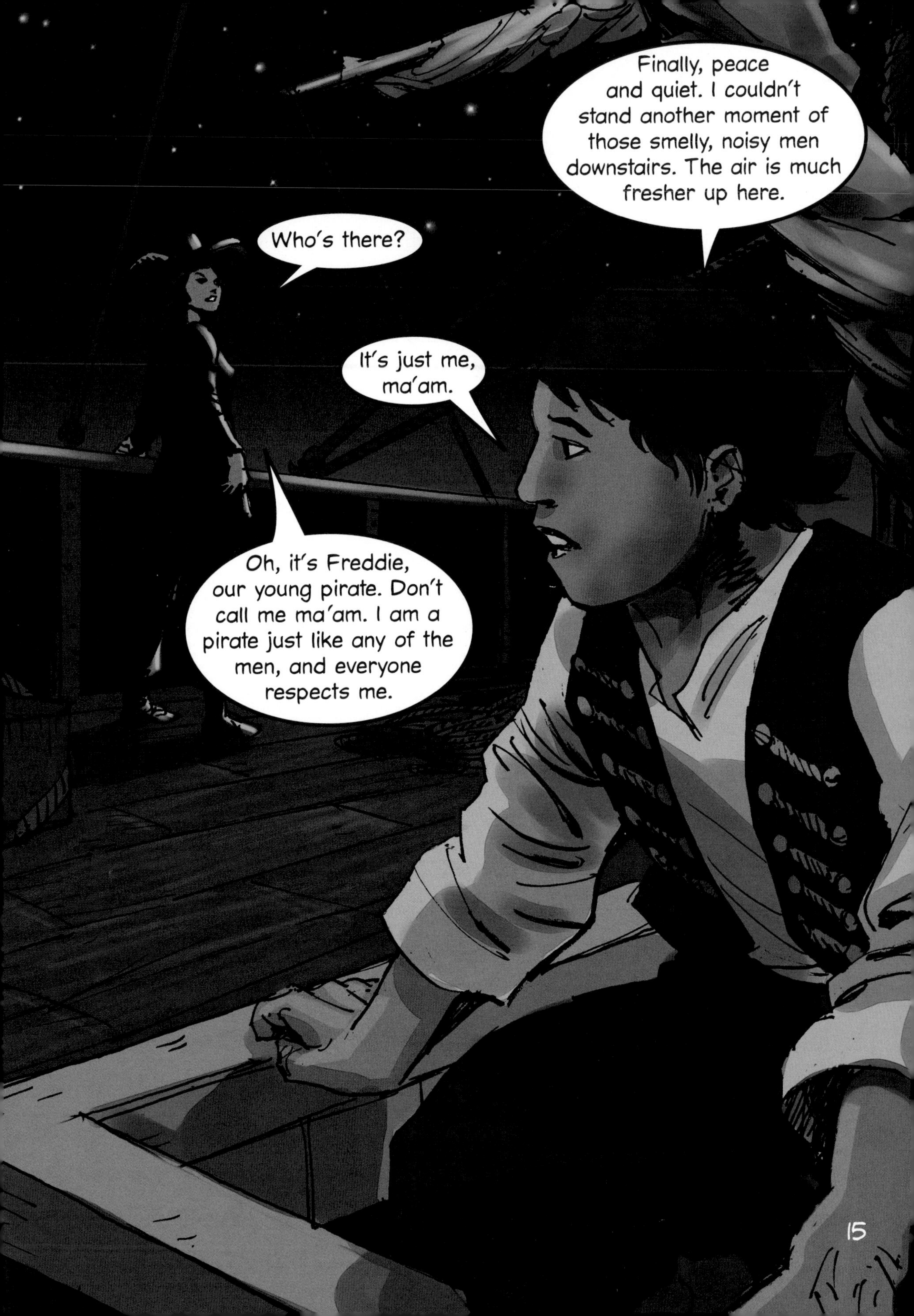
Finally, peace and quiet. I couldn't stand another moment of those smelly, noisy men downstairs. The air is much fresher up here.
Who's there?
It's just me, ma'am.
Oh, it's Freddie, our young pirate. Don't call me ma'am. I am a pirate just like any of the men, and everyone respects me.

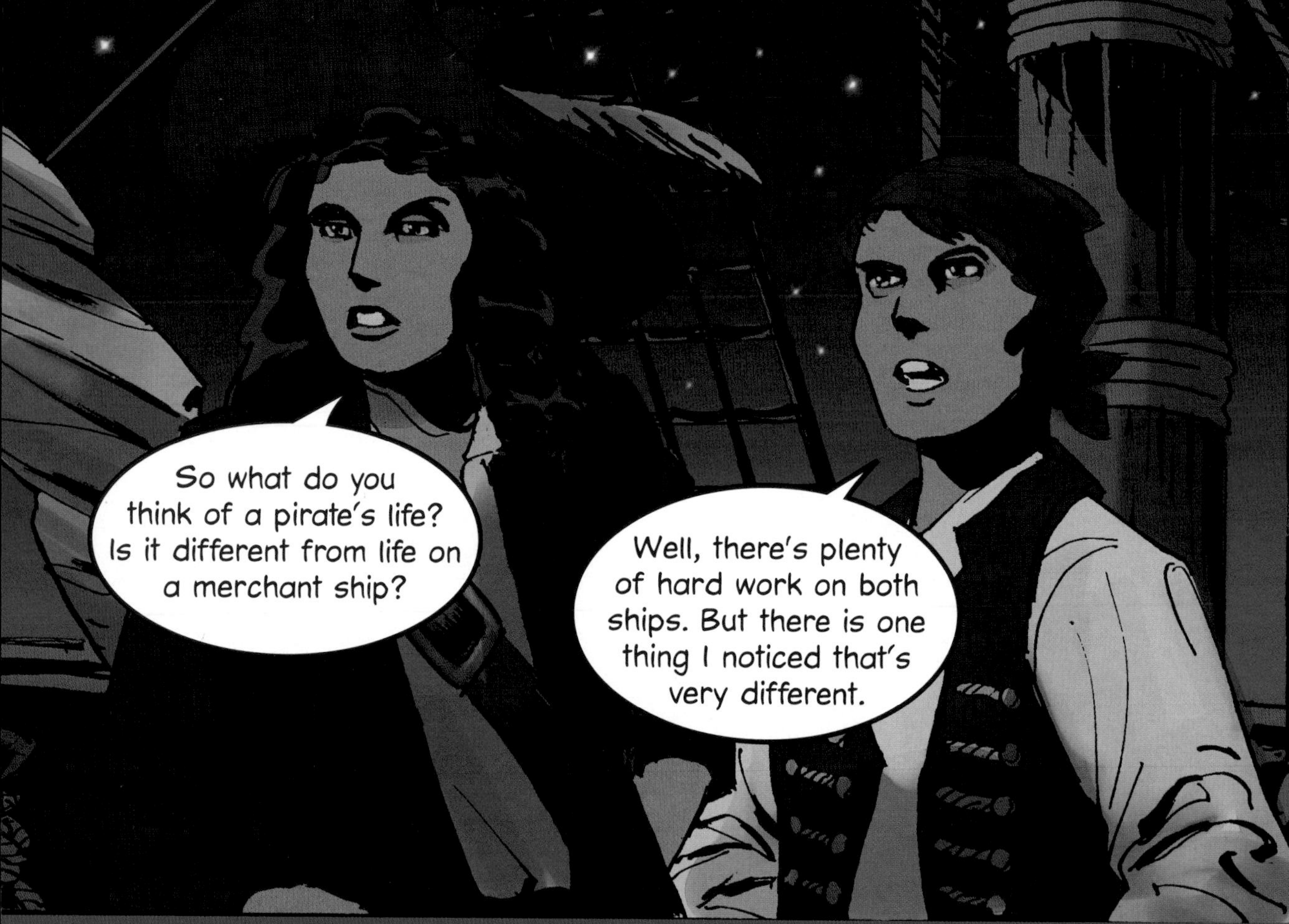
So what do you think of a pirate's life? Is it different from life on a merchant ship?
Well, there's plenty of hard work on both ships. But there is one thing I noticed that's very different.

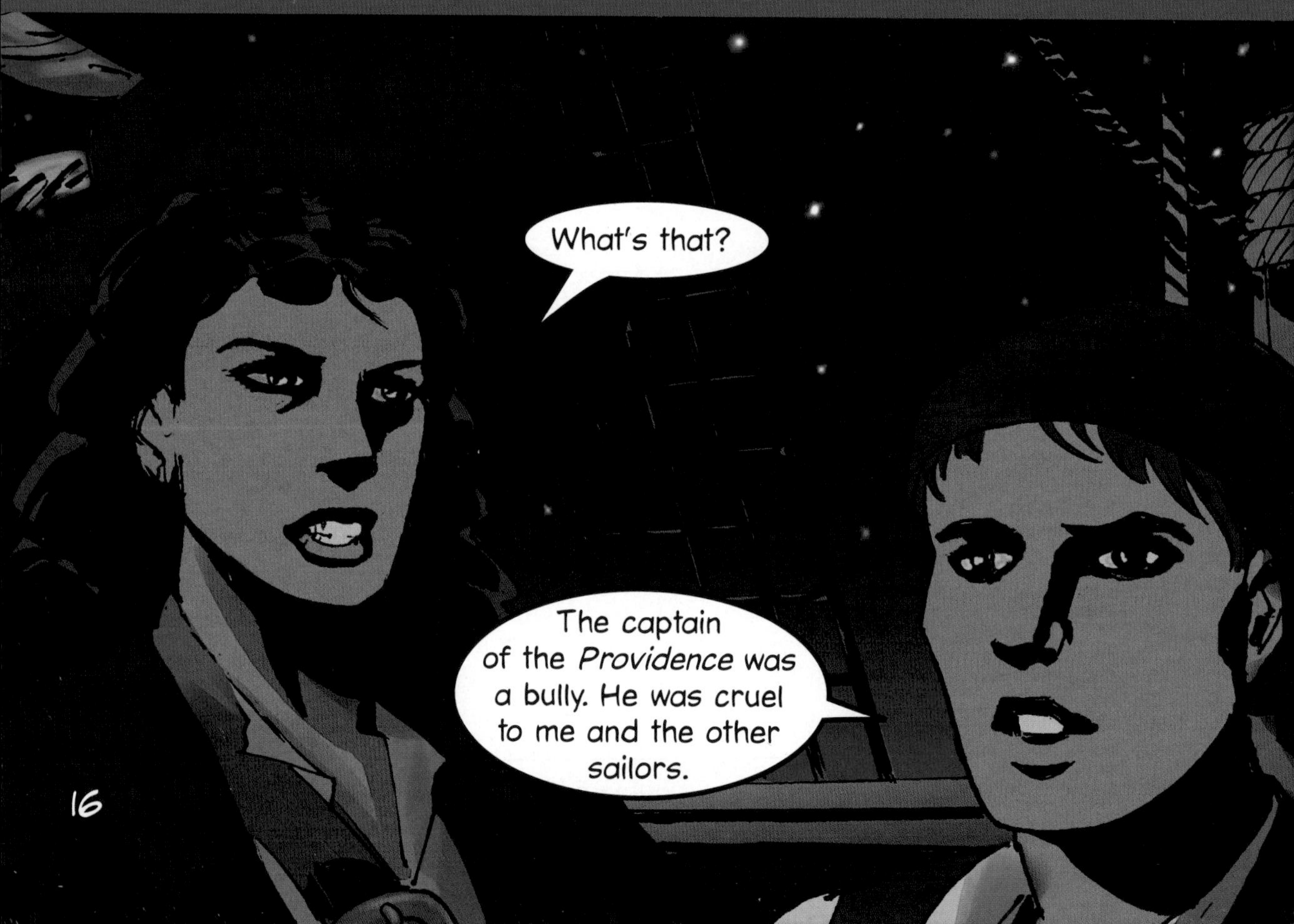
What's that?
The captain of the *Providence* was a bully. He was cruel to me and the other sailors.

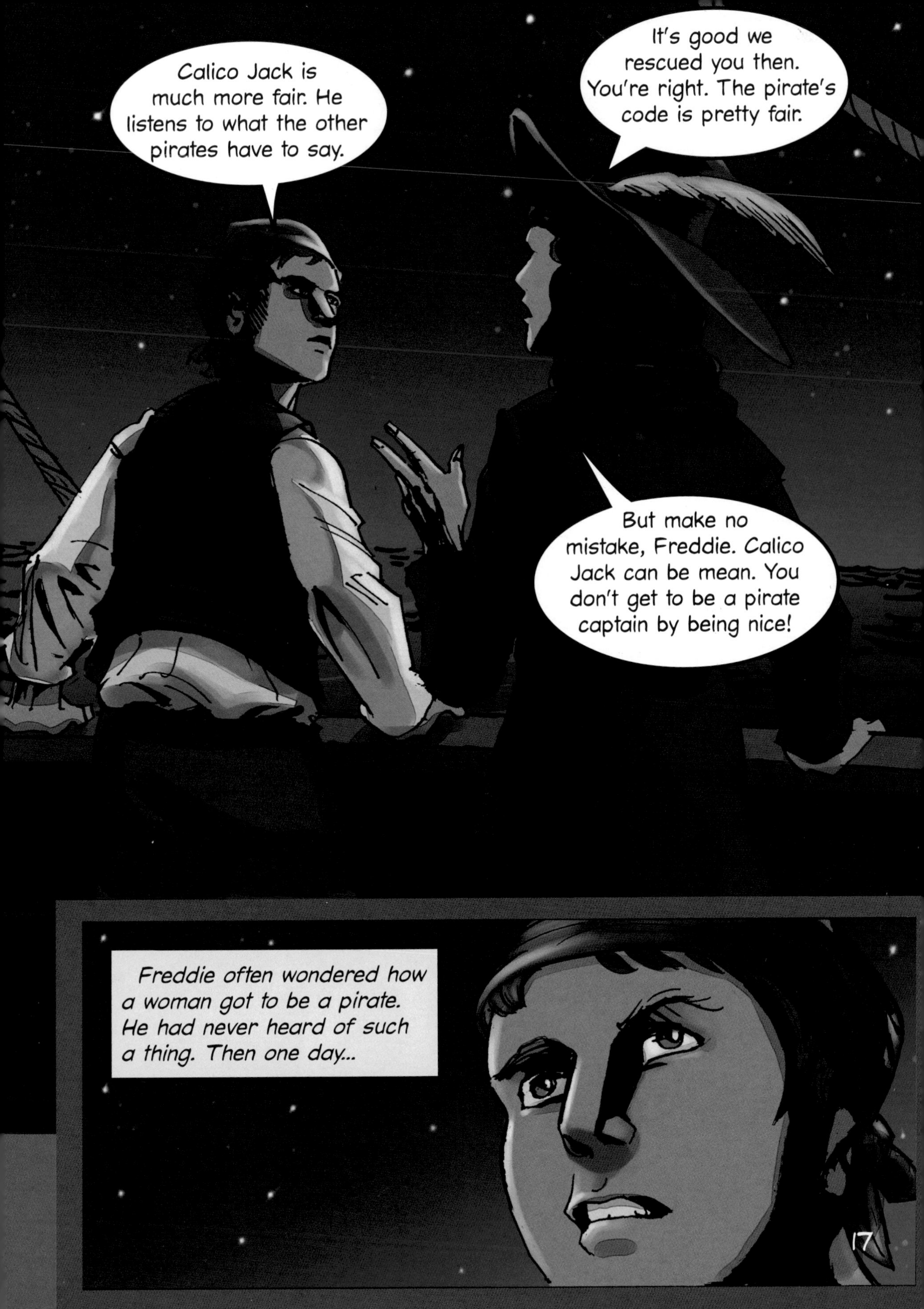

Calico Jack is much more fair. He listens to what the other pirates have to say.
It's good we rescued you then. You're right. The pirate's code is pretty fair.
But make no mistake, Freddie. Calico Jack can be mean. You don't get to be a pirate captain by being nice!
Freddie often wondered how a woman got to be a pirate. He had never heard of such a thing. Then one day...

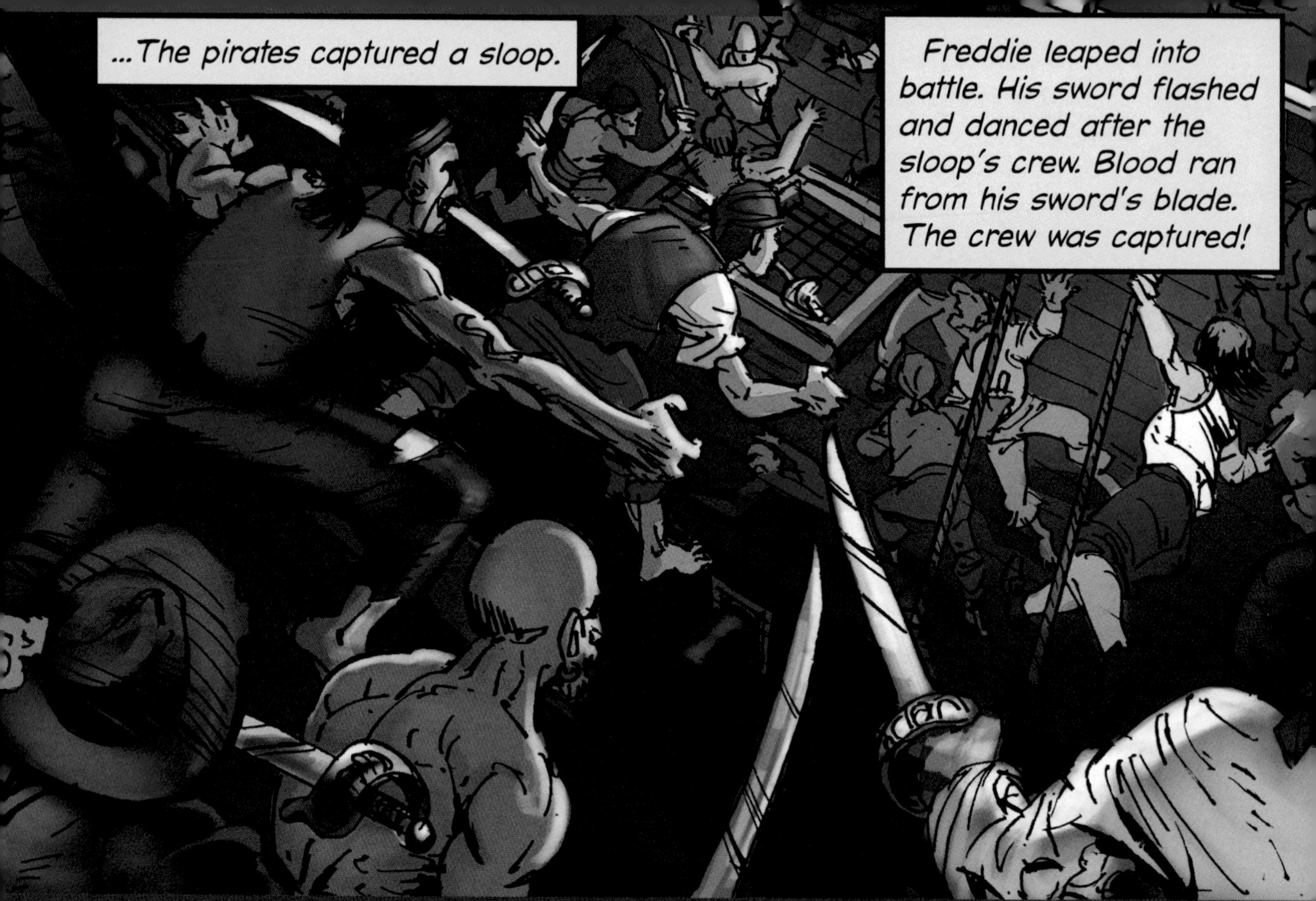
...The pirates captured a sloop.
Freddie leaped into battle. His sword flashed and danced after the sloop's crew. Blood ran from his sword's blade. The crew was captured!

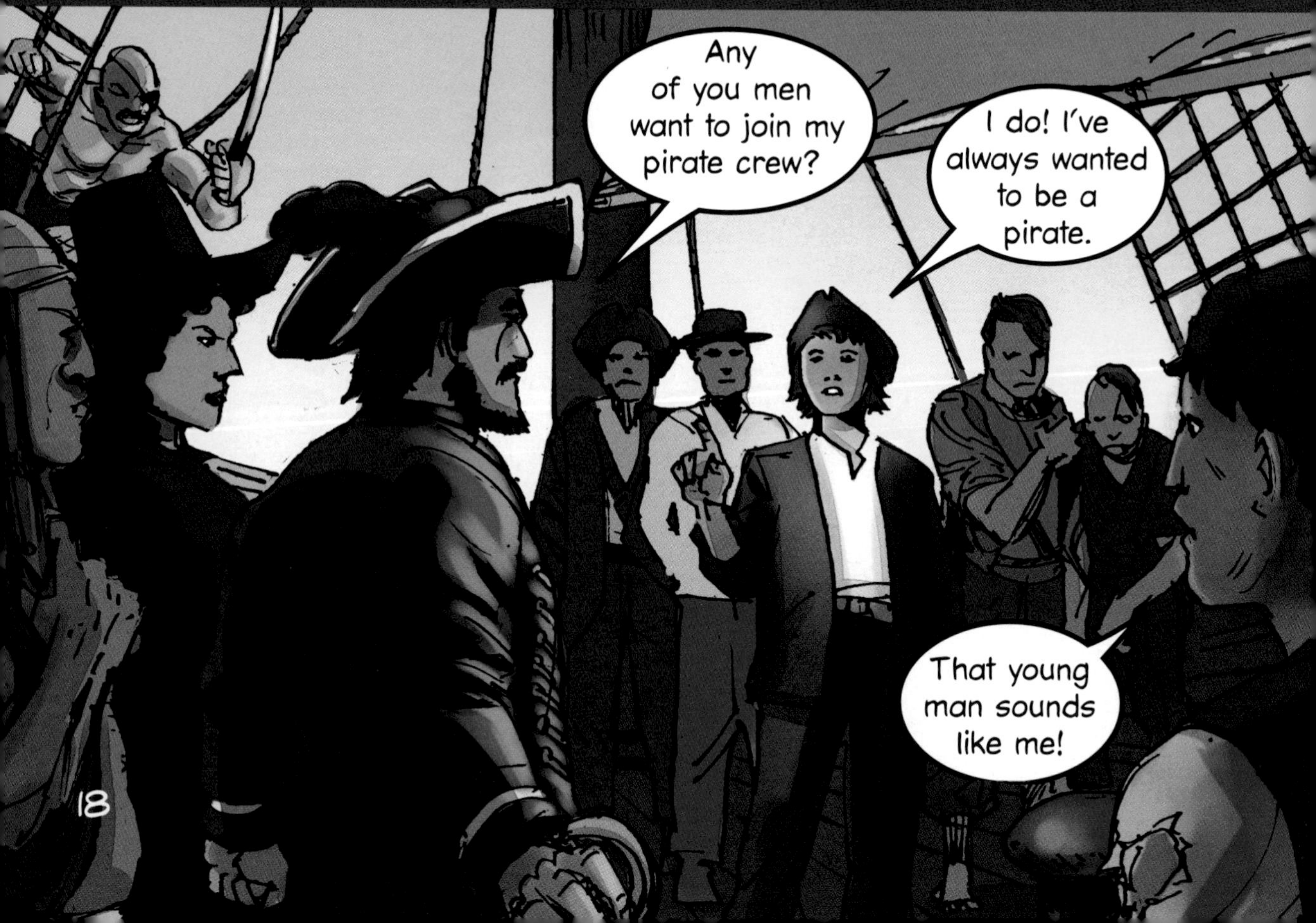
Any of you men want to join my pirate crew?
I do! I've always wanted to be a pirate.
That young man sounds like me!

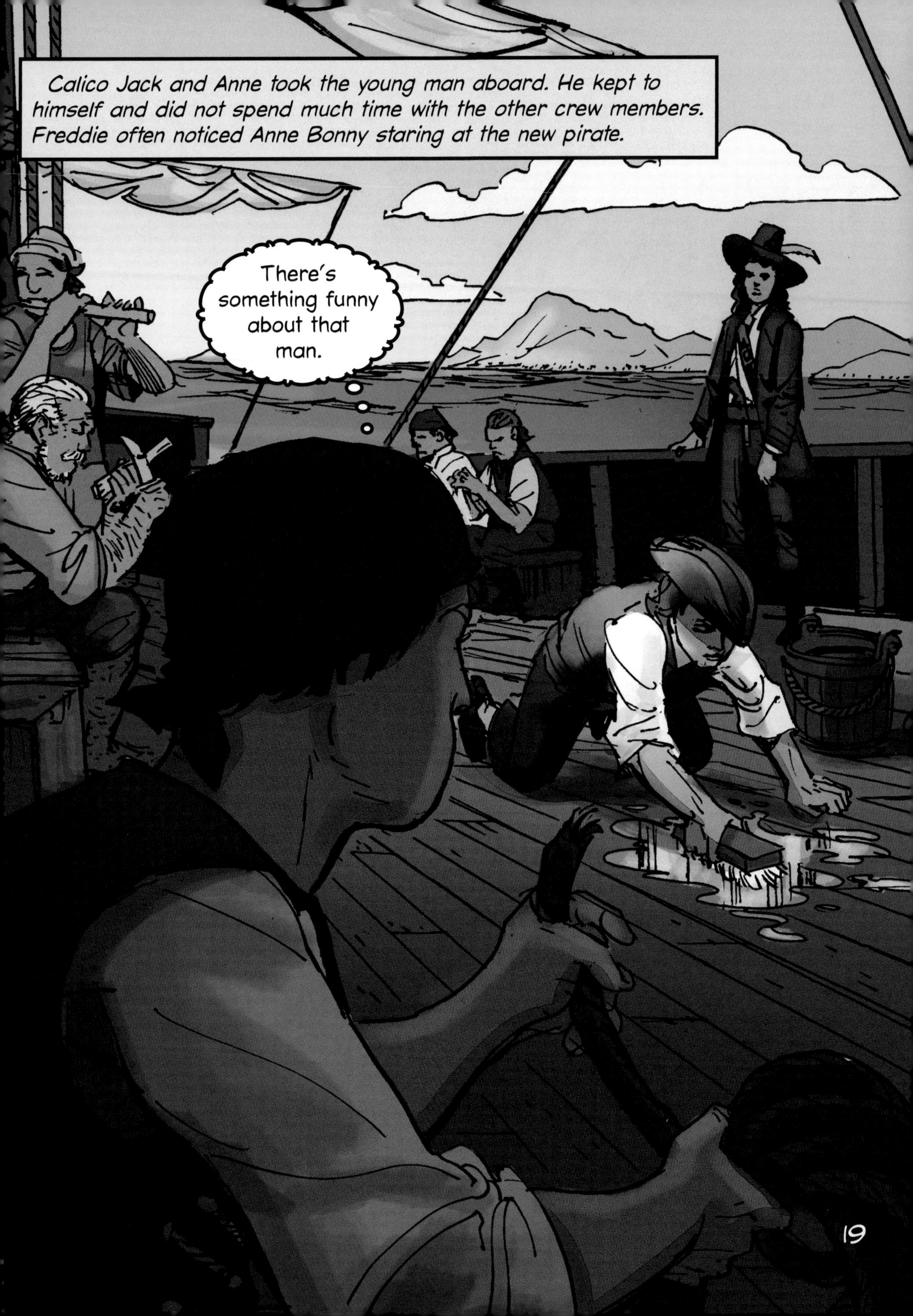
Calico Jack and Anne took the young man aboard. He kept to himself and did not spend much time with the other crew members. Freddie often noticed Anne Bonny staring at the new pirate.
There's something funny about that man.

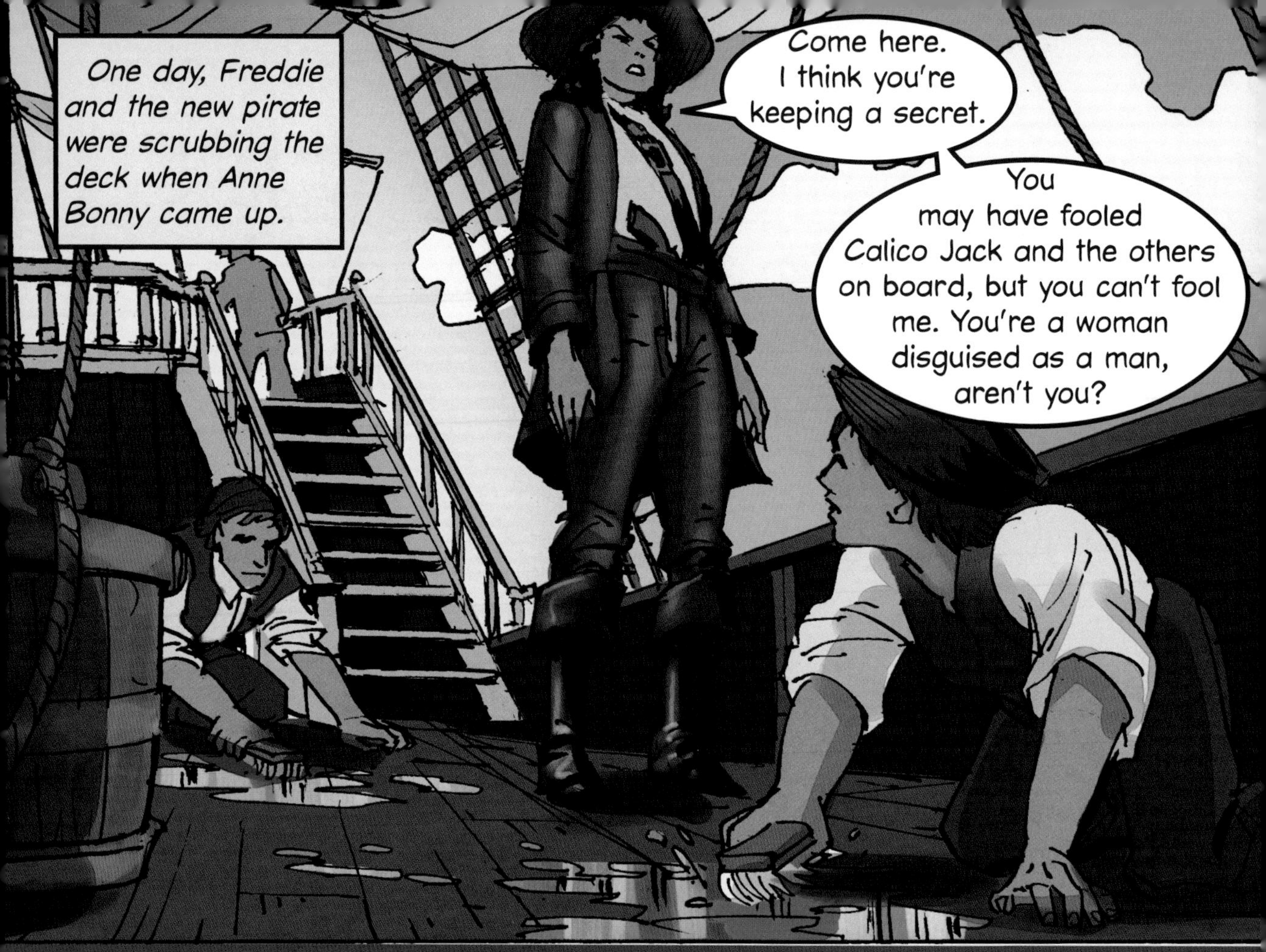
One day, Freddie and the new pirate were scrubbing the deck when Anne Bonny came up.
Come here. I think you're keeping a secret.
You may have fooled Calico Jack and the others on board, but you can't fool me. You're a woman disguised as a man, aren't you?

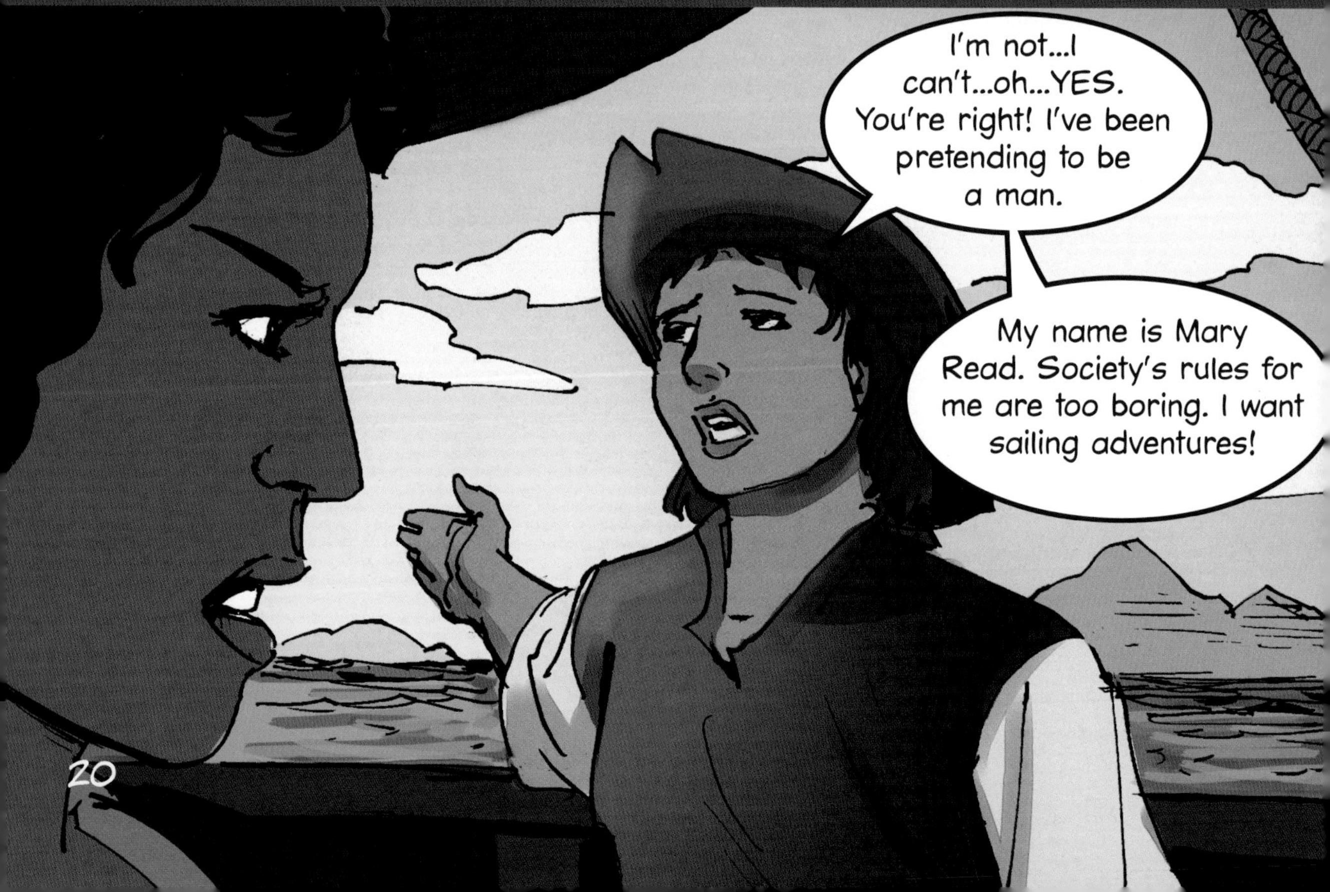
I'm not...I can't...oh...YES. You're right! I've been pretending to be a man.
My name is Mary Read. Society's rules for me are too boring. I want sailing adventures!

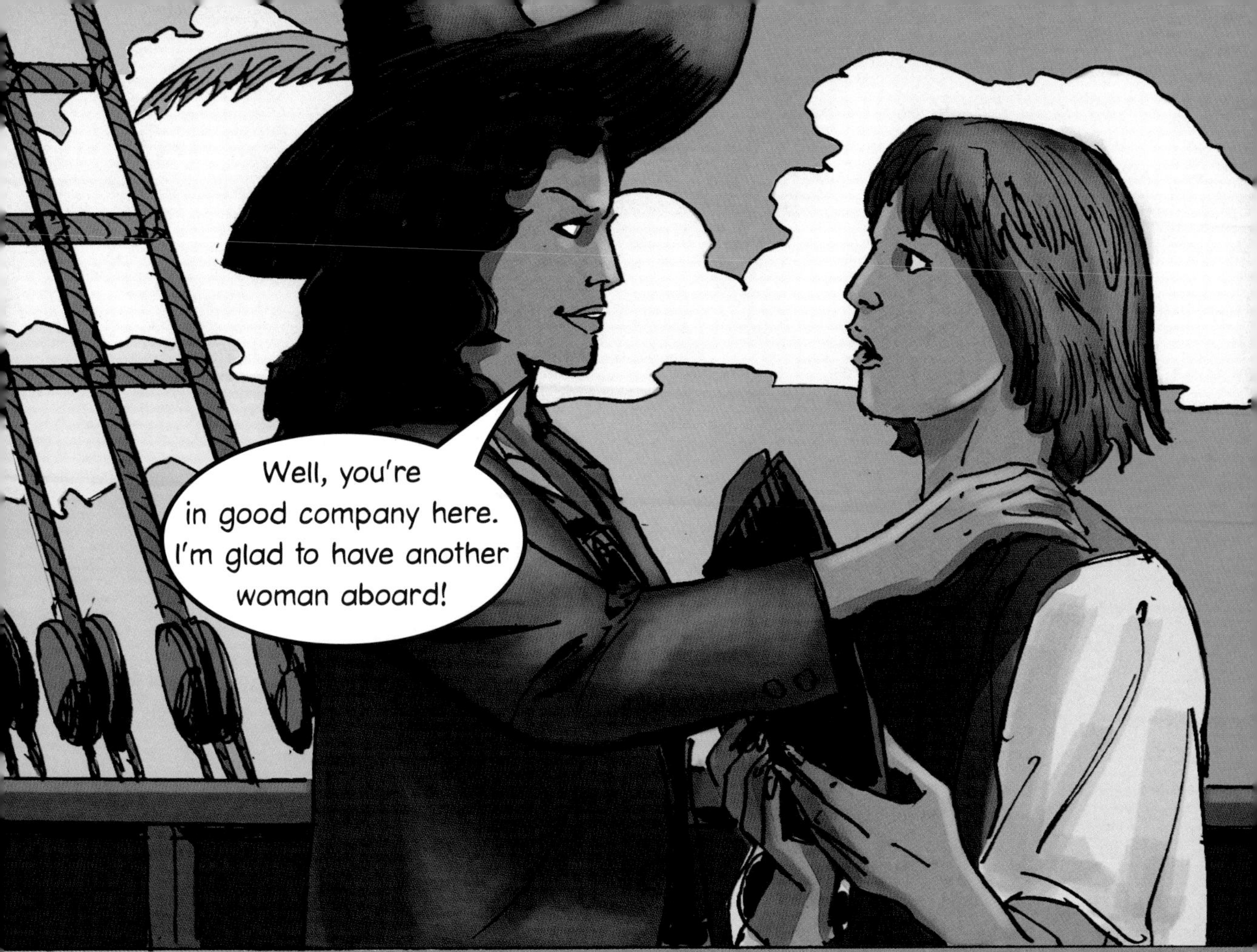
Well, you're in good company here. I'm glad to have another woman aboard!

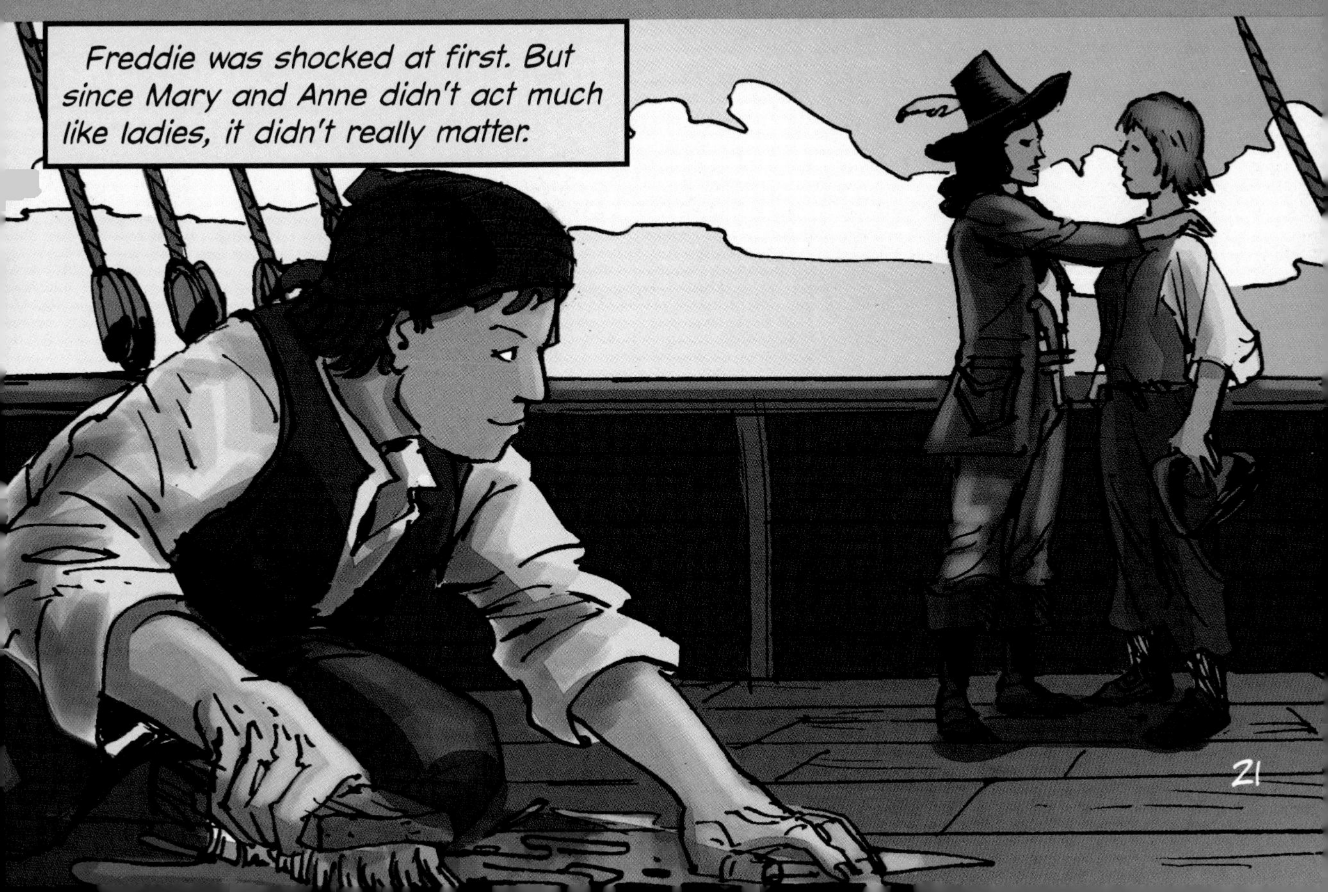
Freddie was shocked at first. But since Mary and Anne didn't act much like ladies, it didn't really matter.

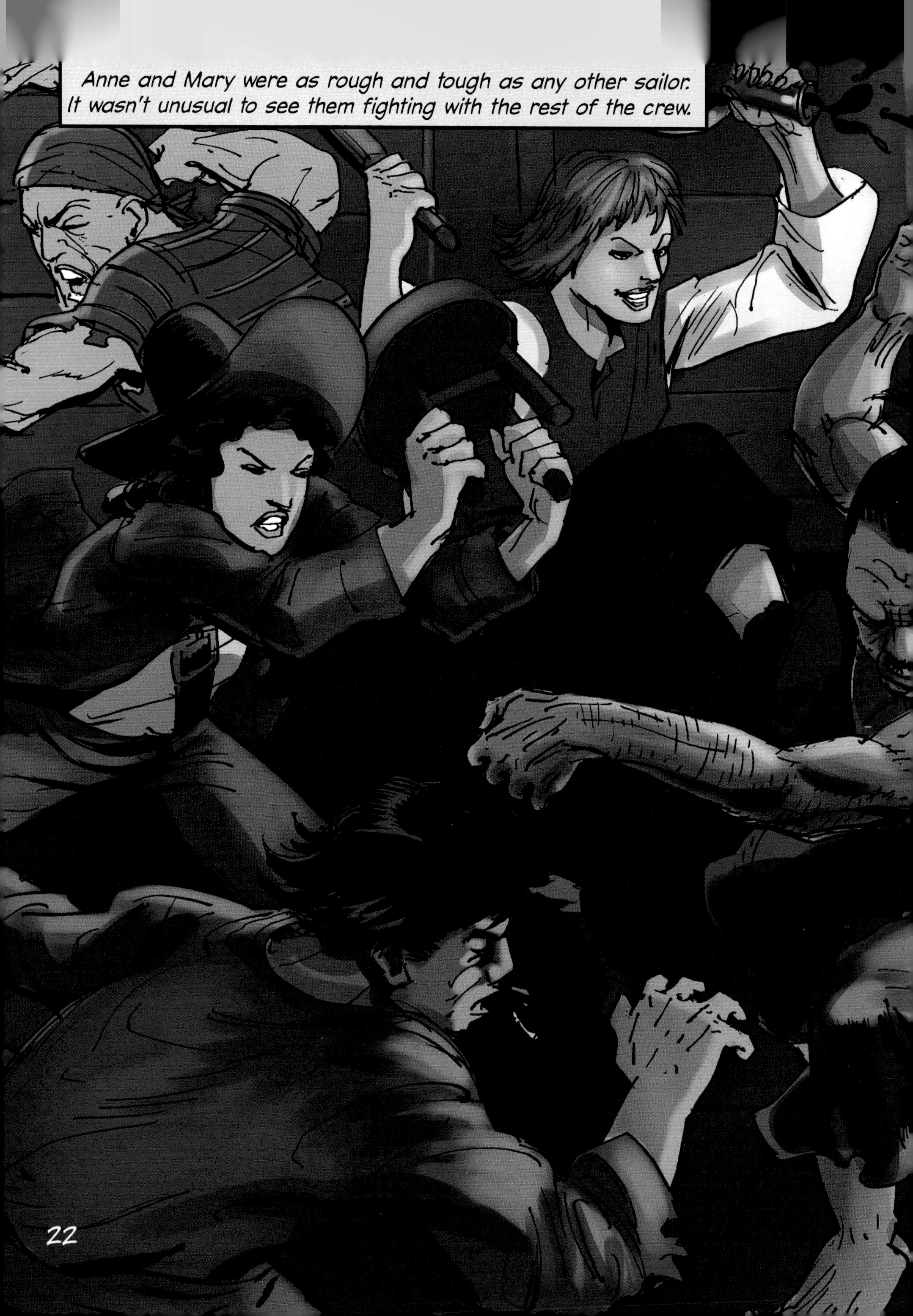
Anne and Mary were as rough and tough as any other sailor. It wasn't unusual to see them fighting with the rest of the crew.

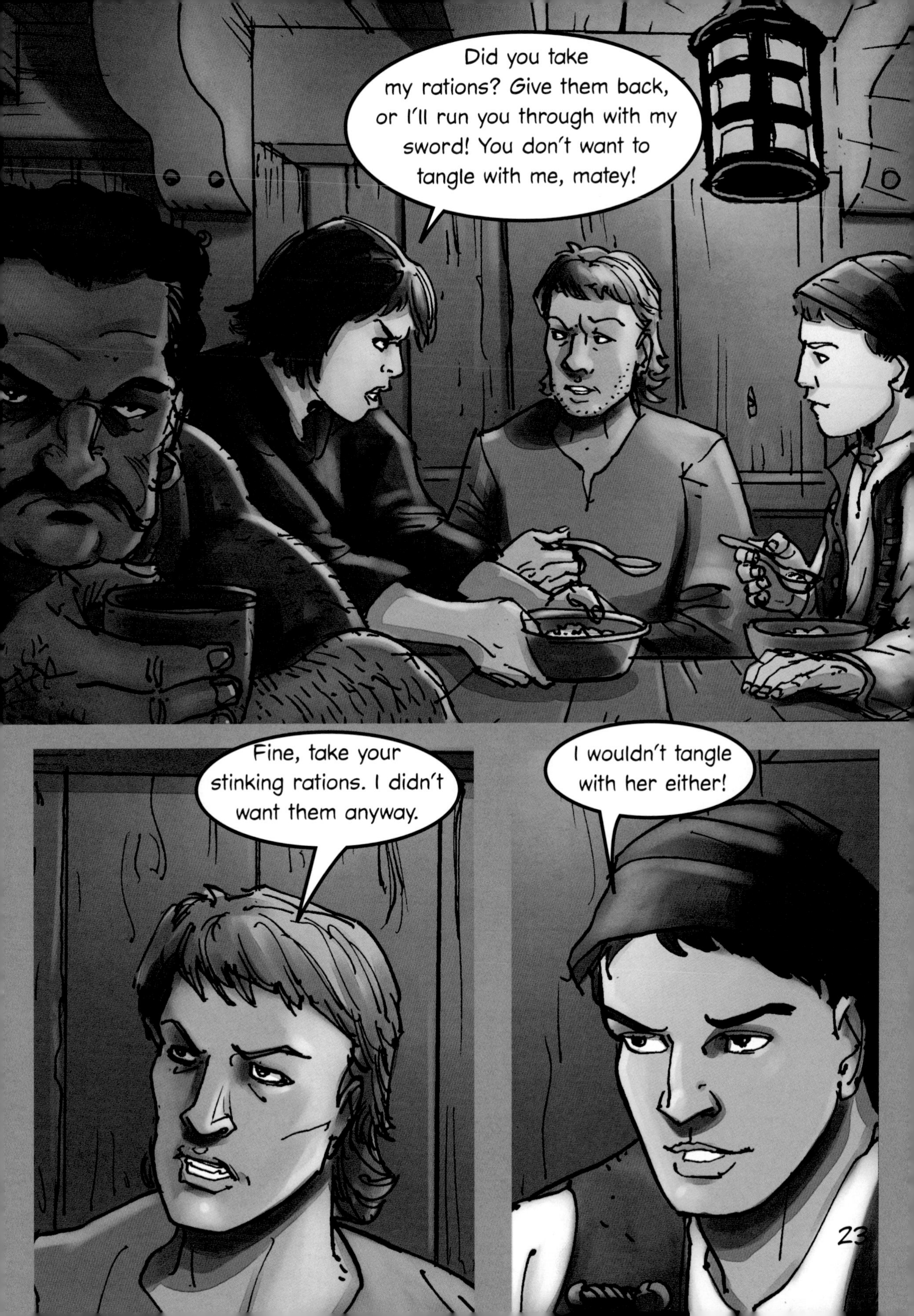
Did you take my rations? Give them back, or I'll run you through with my sword! You don't want to tangle with me, matey!
Fine, take your stinking rations. I didn't want them anyway.
I wouldn't tangle with her either!

# INTO THE UNKNOWN

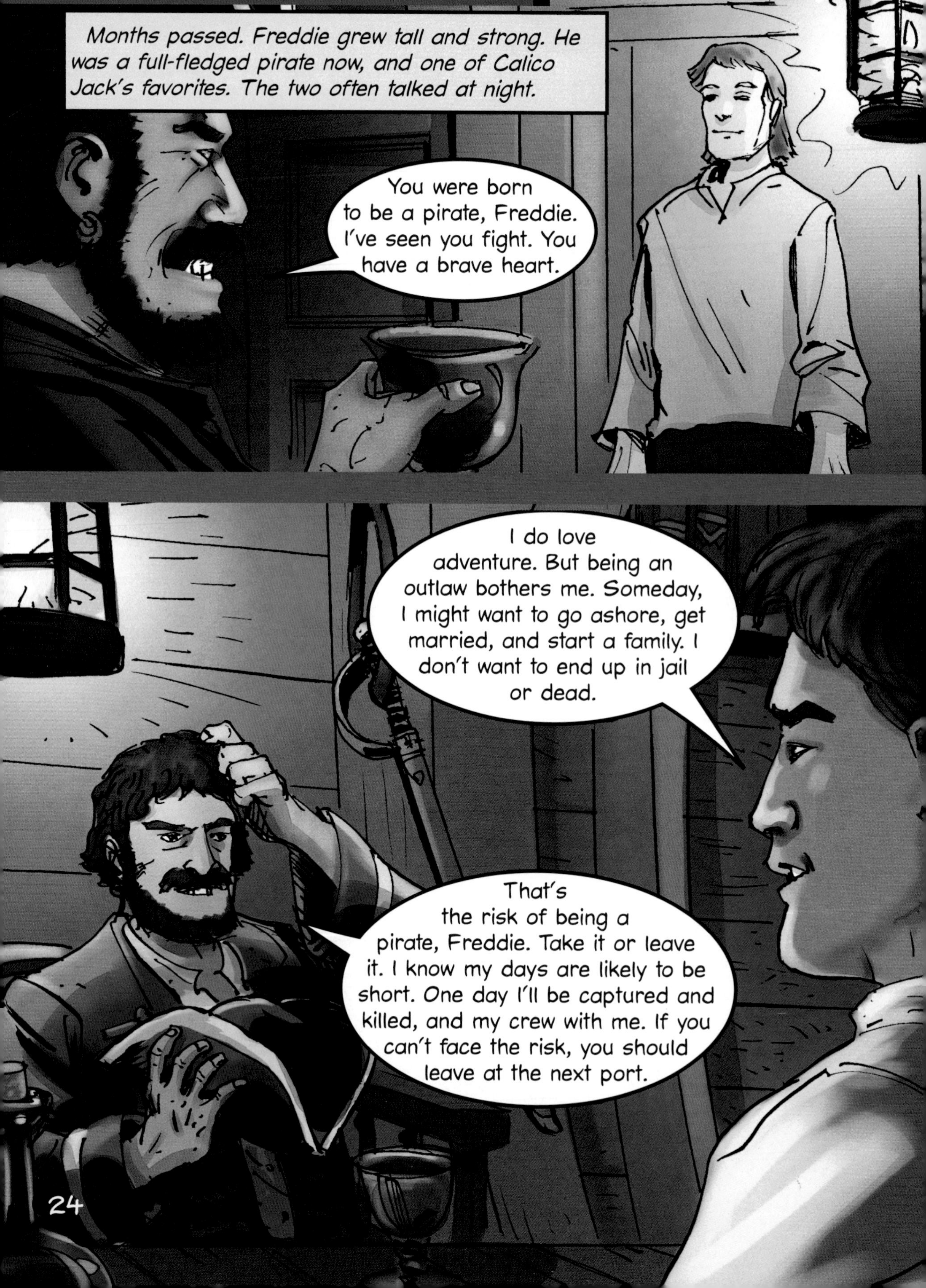
Months passed. Freddie grew tall and strong. He was a full-fledged pirate now, and one of Calico Jack's favorites. The two often talked at night.
You were born to be a pirate, Freddie. I've seen you fight. You have a brave heart.
I do love adventure. But being an outlaw bothers me. Someday, I might want to go ashore, get married, and start a family. I don't want to end up in jail or dead.
That's the risk of being a pirate, Freddie. Take it or leave it. I know my days are likely to be short. One day I'll be captured and killed, and my crew with me. If you can't face the risk, you should leave at the next port.

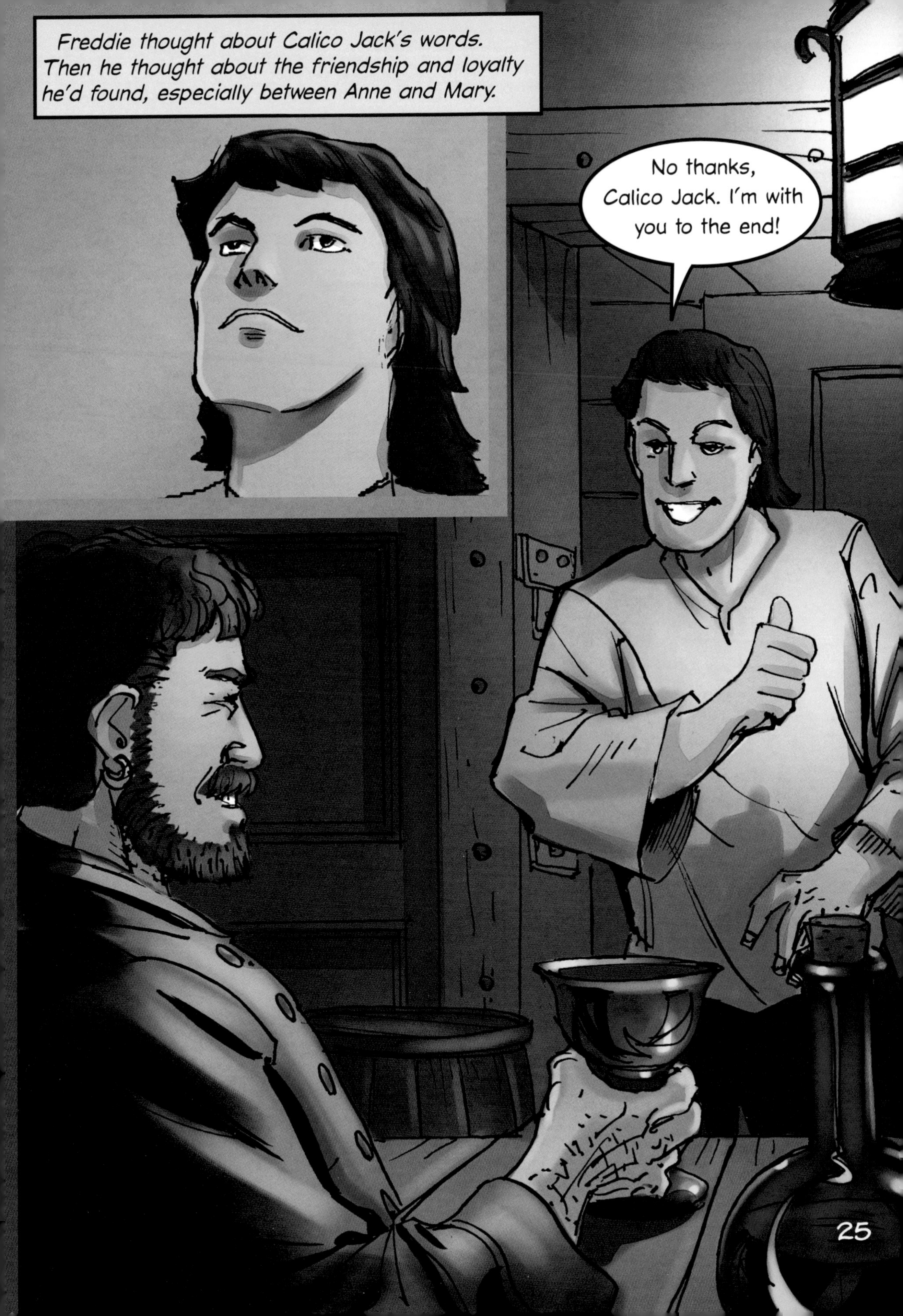
Freddie thought about Calico Jack's words. Then he thought about the friendship and loyalty he'd found, especially between Anne and Mary.
No thanks, Calico Jack. I'm with you to the end!

Pirates have been the terror of the high seas for hundreds of years. These ruthless, violent men and women fought others to claim gold and treasure for themselves.

Pirates were especially common between the sixteenth and eighteenth centuries. At this time, ships were used to trade and send goods back and forth between nations and continents. These ships full of valuables were too tempting for pirates to ignore.

Pirates set sail in their own ships. When they saw a likely target, they opened fire with cannons. Then they tried to board the ship to finish the fight with swords and knives. If they won the battle, pirates took possession of the ship and all of its goods. The unlucky sailors were often killed, taken prisoner, or left behind to die at sea.

*When a pirate ship attacked another vessel, the air filled with cannon fire, gun smoke, and the sounds of fighting.*

## Pirate Treasure

There are many stories of pirates who buried or hid vast amounts of treasure. Many people have used treasure maps to find these hidden collections of gold and jewels. However, most pirates spent their riches as soon as they had them, so there was not much left for others to find.

*Pirates weren't afraid to fight with each other over treasure.*

## Legal Pirates?

Although most pirates were viewed as criminals, some actually won great honor from kings and queens. These pirates worked for the government, and their job was to steal goods from enemy ships. Instead of being called pirates, these seamen were known as **privateers**. Although they shared their treasure with the king or queen, some privateers became very rich and honorable members of society.

## Not Just Men!

Although most pirates were men, women sometimes joined the ranks of the pirates, too. Two of the most famous female pirates were Anne Bonny and Mary Read. Both women lived during the 1700s, and both had a taste for adventure during a time when women were expected to stay home and raise families.

*Anne Bonny was one of the most famous pirates of the Caribbean.*

When Anne Bonny met Jack Rackham (the pirate known as Calico Jack because of his colorful pants), she left her family to join him on his pirate ship, named *Treasure*. Later, Mary Read joined their crew.

Anne, Mary, and Jack spent a short time as pirates in the Caribbean Sea before they were captured and sent to trial. While all of the men were convicted and executed, Anne and Mary were let go because both were expecting babies.

## What Are Pirates Like Today?

Modern day pirates have been attacking cargo ships in recent years off the coast of Somalia, which is in eastern Africa. The pirates usually sail small boats and carry guns to try and force their way onboard the much larger cargo vessels. Once they get onboard, they hold the ship and its crew ransom as they try to extort money from foreign governments in exchange for the ship's release.

Piracy has increased in Somalia in part due to the country having no stable government. The country is very poor and piracy is seen by some Somalis as a way to work for money. Foreign navies have begun patrolling the Indian Ocean near Somalia to make it safer for cargo ships to pass by.

## Websites

www.lucylearns.com/calico-jack.html

www.nationalgeographic.com/pirates

sciway3.net/2001/sc-pirates/index.html

www.isd12.org/BHE/Archives/Activities/Pirates/Bios/
    Rackam/rackam.html

# Glossary

**calico** (KAL-i-koh): This is a cotton cloth printed with a colorful pattern.

**crew** (KROO): These are the group of people who work together on a ship.

**crow's nest** (KROHZ NEST): This is a small platform on the mast of a ship. It is used as a lookout.

**merchant** (MUR-chuhnt): This is a person who buys and sells goods.

**privateers** (prye-vi-TIHRZ): These are pirates who had government permission to capture enemy ships.

**rations** (RASH-uhnz): This is a small share of food.

**sloop** (SLOOP): This a sailboat with one mast.

**starboard** (STAR-burd): This is the right side of a ship.

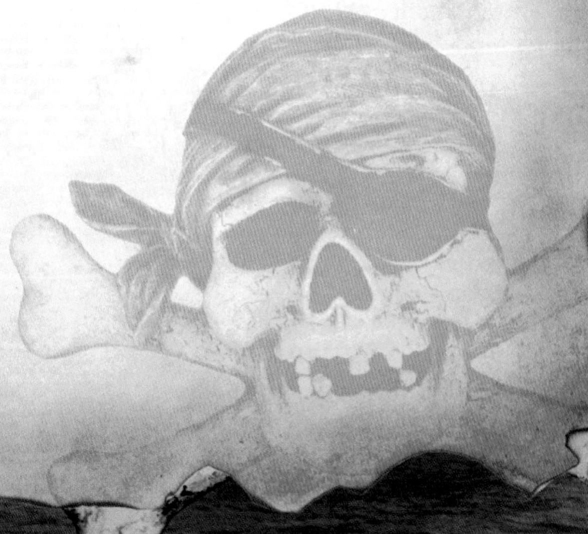

# Index

# About the Author

Joanne Mattern is the author of more than 300 books for children. She has written about a variety of subjects, including sports, history, biography, animals, and science. She loves bringing nonfiction subjects to life for children! Joanne lives in New York state with her husband, four children, and assorted pets.

# About the Artist

Chris Marrinan is an artist who has created images for many things, including everything from billboards to video game covers! He got his start in the comic book business drawing for comic book publishers DC Comics, Marvel, Dark Horse, and Image. Chris has drawn many comic icons, such as Wonder Woman, Spider-Man, and Wolverine. He lives in Northern California with his two children.